100 Questions and Answers About U.S. Catholics

Pope Francis, his Legacy and
the Transition to Pope Leo XIV

**Michigan State University
School of Journalism**

Front Edge Publishing

For more information and further discussion, visit

biasbusterguides.com

Cover design by Rick Nease
RickNeaseArt.com

Published by
Front Edge Publishing
42807 Ford Road, #234
Canton, Michigan, 48187

Front Edge Publishing books are available for discount bulk purchases for events, corporate use and small groups. Special editions, including books with corporate logos, personalized covers and customized interiors are available for purchase. For more information, contact Front Edge Publishing at info@FrontEdgePublishing.com

Contents

Acknowledgments

These are the authors of this Bias Busters guide, from left: Sabrina Boxer, Emile Rizk, Lacie Kunselman, Nicoline Bradford, Karlyn Kelley, Angelina Sandora, Heather Araj, Mark Krueger-Vanoyen, Shelby Frink, Madison Scanlon, Yu-An (Annie) Fan Chiang, Samantha Bluga, Ben Walker, Hailey Woodworth and Addison Carter. Also: Jack Foster. Kunselman and Michigan State graduate Debrah Miszak took the edits over the finish line. Kunselman works in logistics for The TJX Companies, Inc., in Massachusetts. Miszak has been published in The Forward, Tikkun, National Catholic Reporter and U.S. Catholic.

This guide was helped by several allies.

Father Gordon Reigle, pastor, and **Katie Diller Gleason**, director of campus ministry, introduced the class to East Lansing's St. John Church and Student Center, which are affiliated with St. Thomas Aquinas parish.

Michigan Hall of Fame journalist and author **Patricia Montemurri** spoke to the class over Zoom and critiqued drafts of the guide. In her 36 years as a reporter with the Detroit Free Press, Montemurri often covered news about Catholics and popes. She is the author of "Detroit Gesu Catholic Church and School," "Blessed Solanus Casey," "Immaculate Heart of Mary Sisters of Michigan," "Mercy High School of Michigan" and "Ss. Peter and Paul Jesuit: Detroit's Oldest Church."

Mike Stechschulte, managing editor of The Michigan Catholic from 2012-2018 and editor-in-chief of its online successor, Detroit Catholic, advised and critiqued the guide.

Bill Mitchell, former National Catholic Reporter CEO and publisher, encouraged us to take up this project and advised us. He has a bachelor's degree in theology from Notre Dame University and has been a journalist and educator for 50 years.

Editing allies include **Sister Erin McDonald**, CSJ, digital youth minister for the congregation of St. Joseph and a host of the Beyond the Habit podcast. She previously served as university minister for service and social justice at the University of Detroit Mercy and as a case manager at Freedom House Detroit. Another ally has been **Sister Jane Aseltyne**, IHM. She has been accepted into the PhD program in Integrative Studies in Ethics and Theology at Loyola University Chicago.

Sister Maria Inviolata and **Sister Mary Philomena** of the Sisters of Our Mother of Divine Grace, established under the Second Vatican Council and based in Port Sanilac, Michigan, advised and critiqued the guide.

Many times, the authors turned to the **United States Conference of Catholic Bishops**, the **Center for Applied Research in the Apostolate** at Georgetown University, the **Pew Research Center** and the **National Catholic Reporter**.

Thanks to Michigan State School of Journalism professor **Richard Epps**, whose graphics students produced charts for this guide.

Finally, we wish to thank MSU School of Journalism professor and Director **Tim P. Vos**, PhD., for his support of the Bias Busters series.

Foreword

By the Most Rev. Walter A. Hurley

The Catholic Church is about building the kingdom of God. Its many doctrines, beliefs, practices and structures are meant to promote that kingdom and serve God's people in their following of Christ. The very complex reality of the church we have today has evolved over the centuries. The church has been led by human persons and is not without great success and blessing and at the same time failure and sin over the ages. Catholics believe that the Holy Spirit guides and directs the church in the midst of human failure and sinfulness.

In our day, the Second Vatican Council (1962-1965) has been a dominant force seeking to renew various aspects of the life of the church. The implementation of the council has not been without its challenges for Catholics today. It has involved significant changes and renewal in structure and practice. The council generally has been widely embraced by the Catholic community. In recent years, however, the sex-abuse scandal has seriously damaged the reputation of leadership in the Church in its response to that crisis.

As we read in this book the various answers that have been prepared to many of the practical questions it is useful not to lose sight of the big picture. Who are the members and leaders who make up the Catholic Church and the task they undertake?

A reflection written by Bishop Kenneth Untener, of the Diocese of Saginaw, Michigan (1980-2004) but commonly attributed to Saint Oscar Romero, the martyred archbishop of San Salvador (Feb. 11, 1977-March 24, 1980) is worthy of our reflection as we read of the various practical questions that arise regarding the Catholic Church and its mission and members.

The beliefs, practices and structures of the Roman Catholic Church, having evolved over the centuries, give rise to a variety of questions regarding current belief and practice of Roman Catholics.

Bishop Untener wrote:

"It helps, now and then, to step back and take the long view. The Kingdom is not only beyond our efforts; it is even beyond our vision. We accomplish in our lifetime only a fraction of the magnificent enterprise that is God's work. Nothing we do is complete, which is another way of saying the Kingdom always lies beyond us.

"No statement says all that could be said. No prayer fully expresses our faith. No confession brings perfection. No pastoral visit brings wholeness. No program accomplishes the church's mission. No set of goals and objectives includes everything. This is what we are about.

"We plant the seeds that one day will grow. We water the seeds that are already planted, knowing that they hold future promise. We lay foundations that will need further development. We provide yeast that produces effects far beyond our capabilities.

"We cannot do everything and there is a sense of liberation in realizing that. This enables us to do something and do it well. It may be incomplete, but is a beginning, a step along the way, an opportunity for the Lord's grace to enter and do the rest. We may never see the end results, but that is the difference between the master builder and the worker. We are workers, not master builders, not messiahs.

"We are prophets of a future not our own."

Pope Francis, left, and Bishop Hurley talk. Vatican photo.

The Most Rev. Bishop Walter A. Hurley is currently the Bishop Emeritus of the Diocese of Grand Rapids, having served as bishop from Aug. 4, 2005, to June 18, 2013. He was appointed by Pope Benedict XVI.

From Aug. 11, 2003, until his appointment to Grand Rapids, Hurley served as Auxiliary Bishop in the Archdiocese of Detroit. Following his retirement as Bishop of Grand Rapids, he served as Apostolic Administrator of the Diocese of Saginaw, Michigan (Oct. 17, 2018 to July 26, 2019) and then the Diocese of Gaylord, Michigan (June 23, 2020 to March 4, 2022).

Ordained a priest June 5, 1965, Hurley served in various parishes in the Archdiocese of Detroit. Following graduate work at the Catholic University of America (JCL degree in canon law) he served as Judicial Vicar and Moderator of the Curia of the Archdiocese. He served as Cardinal Szoka's and later Cardinal Maida's delegate for clergy misconduct. He was the project manager for the construction of the Pope John Paul II Cultural Center in Washington, D.C.

Bishop Hurley brings a broad background in pastoral care and administration over the many years as priest and bishop.

Introduction

By Bill Tammeus

The small town in which I grew up after World War II, Woodstock, Illinois, northwest of Chicago, was a landslide for Christianity. Which, of course, meant it was a religiously atomized community. There were lots of different kinds of Protestants, including members of the Presbyterian church to which my family belonged. But there also were enough Catholics to support not just a large church but also an elementary school and eventually an excellent high school. And there was a pretty little Christian Science church not far from Woodstock's central square.

If there was theological and biblical illiteracy in the pews of all those churches (and there was), there also was plenty of ignorance about what people outside of one's own congregation believed and how they worshiped. Had this book been available back in the 1950s and onward, it might have gone a long way toward unplugging ignorance as well as the prejudice that seems almost inevitably to sprout in the soil of religious illiteracy.

The problem of theological ignorance and bias is not, of course, limited to Christians. Religious illiteracy seems not just rampant in the U.S. but also growing even as the American religious landscape undergoes some major changes. Since President Lyndon B. Johnson signed immigration reform into law in 1965, lots of people from around the world have come to our shores, bringing with them their religious traditions, including Hinduism, Buddhism, Islam, Sikhism and others. At the same time, the portion of the adult American population identifying as religiously unaffiliated has grown close to 30 percent while American Christianity has suffered obvious diminishment.

The result has been a need for exactly the kind of book you hold in your hands. And the sooner there are similar books to help people understand every religious tradition, the better. We know, after all, that ignorance produces fear, which can produce extremism, which can produce violence. I have addressed exactly that problem in my latest book, "Love, Loss and Endurance: A 9/11 Story of Resilience and Hope in an Age of Anxiety." It tells the story of the countless traumas my extended family suffered because terrorists murdered my nephew, a passenger on the first plane to smash into the World Trade Center. Beyond that, it explores how people get drawn into extremism and what we can do about it. One thing we can do about ignorance is replace it with education and understanding. Thus, this book.

Because I've spent many years as a journalist writing about various faith traditions, I didn't expect to learn much in this book about Catholicism. I was wrong. And I'm glad to be wrong — just as you will be glad to learn much more about Catholicism (even if you're Catholic). What all of us must remember is that no matter what faith tradition we pledge allegiance to, we share a common humanity. That should move us not to bigotry but to respect and, better yet, to love. This book will help.

Bill Tammeus is a journalist, blogger and author or co-author of seven books, including "Jesus, Pope Francis and a Protestant Walk into a Bar: Lessons for the Christian Church." For decades Tammeus has written columns for the Kansas City Star, The Presbyterian Outlook and the National Catholic Reporter.

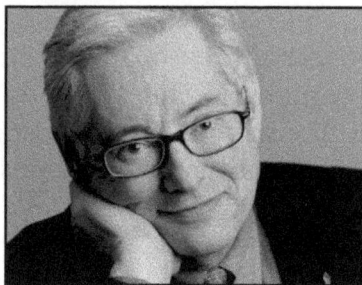

Preface: Transition to Pope Leo XIV

By Joe Grimm

The first pope from the United States, Leo XIV was elected while this book was in production. So, we recount Pope Francis' last, busy years and his influence on the selection of his successor. Some refer to Leo XIV as "Francis II." Others say he will act on his own.

Pope Leo made his intentions clear immediately. In his first Vatican address, he said he would maintain Pope Francis' direction. That includes missionary work, engaging the world and "loving care for the least and the rejected." Leo opposed wars, supported children and immigrants and called on Catholics to serve.

In his first papal Mass, Leo announced his support for the reforms of the 60-year-old Second Vatican Council, which this guide explores, and social justice in the face of artificial intelligence.

More clues about where Leo XIV is coming from and where he'll take the church:

His name: The pope said he chose the name of Leo XIII, pope in 1878-1903, for his emphasis on workers and social issues.

Values: Leo XIV is the first Augustinian friar to become pope. The small order, dating back to 1244, has several values. They include love for God and neighbor, self-reflection to discern God's truth, humility, unity, pursuit of wisdom, freedom and bettering society.

Social issues: For years, Leo worked with poor communities in Peru. He is expected to lean progressively on social issues such as migration and poverty but align more with moderates on moral doctrine and LGBTQ rights. Leo added three women to the office that reviews candidates for bishop, but he has opposed ordaining women.

Key dates: Sept. 14, 1955, born Robert Francis Prevost in Chicago; 1979, graduated from Villanova in Pennsylvania with a degree in mathematics; 1982, ordained as priest in Rome; 1985, assigned to Augustinian missions in Peru where he taught and built parishes; 2015, Pope Francis appointed Leo to work with church hierarchy, made him an archbishop and then a cardinal; May 8, 2025, elected pope.

International: Leo's life spans and unites the Americas. He has spent about 30 years in the United States, about 30 years in Peru and several in Rome. He has U.S. and Peruvian citizenships. He speaks English, Spanish, Italian, French and Portuguese. He can read Latin and Greek. The new pope is at home in Chicago, Illinois, and Chiclayo, Peru, 3,420 miles apart. Both cities are known for architecture and beaches, but their seasons are opposite.

Family: Leo XIV's father was of French and Italian descent; his mother was of Spanish descent. ABC News reports that several census documents describe his mother's parents as Black or mulatto. Those descriptions were changed to White after they moved to Chicago.

Pursuits: Tennis, singing at Mass, Wordle, the Chicago White Sox, high school yearbook editor-in-chief.

Joe Grimm
Series founder and editor
Visiting editor in residence
Michigan State University School of Journalism

Glossary

Advent The season in which Roman Catholics and many Protestants prepare for Christmas. It begins with the Sunday closest to Nov. 30 and ends on Christmas Eve. Eastern Orthodox Christians celebrate the Nativity Fast from Nov. 15 through Dec. 24.

Annunciation Angel Gabriel's announcement to Mary that she would conceive a son, Jesus, who would be the Son of God.

archdiocese A district or area that is larger than a diocese. Location, historical significance or a large population of Catholics give an archdiocese added significance. An archdiocese is led by an archbishop; a diocese is led by a bishop. In the United States there are 144 Latin Catholic dioceses and 33 archdioceses. There are also 16 Eastern Catholic dioceses and two such archdioceses. Additionally, there is an archdiocese for the U.S. military services and a personal ordinariate of the Chair of Saint Peter.

bishop Bishops are regarded as successors of the 12 apostles sent out by Jesus. They typically have spiritual authority over a local diocese and its priests. Some bishops have administrative roles with the church. A primary diocesan bishop may have auxiliary bishops. There are about 5,500 Roman Catholic bishops in the world. A bishop can become an archbishop, cardinal or pope.

brother A man who has taken vows but who is not ordained and who may or may not be studying for the priesthood. Some priests in training are called brothers, but other brothers have chosen the role of brother as a permanent, non-ordained way to live their religious life. Brothers may not administer sacraments. Some brothers take the vow of poverty in addition to vows of celibacy and obedience. They belong to religious orders or congregations of men. Some orders, such as the Society of Jesus (Jesuits), include both brothers and priests. Pope Francis was ordained as a Jesuit priest. Some orders emphasize teaching. Although brothers refers to both monks and friars, it does not apply to those who have been ordained as priests. (Please see friar and monk entries.)

canon Church law, also scriptures the church recognizes as being inspired by the Holy Spirit.

catechism A text that lays out the church's fundamental, universal teachings in a question-and-answer form. The major one used today is the 1992 "Catechism of the Catholic Church." The "Baltimore Catechism," published in 1885, was widely used for Catholic children.

catechumen Convert being trained in discipline and doctrine to prepare for baptism.

celibacy, chastity The first means to abstain from marriage and sexual acts. The second is to live chaste lives, no matter their station. For married people, chastity means fidelity to one's spouse.

College of Cardinals The pope chooses these "princes of the church" as advisers. Most lead dioceses, archdioceses and missions around the world. Others have been Vatican officials, priests and monsignors. Members of the college under the age of 80 are eligible to select popes.

consubstantial The belief that the Father, the Son and the Holy Spirit are of one essence.

creed An official statement of a Christian faith's specific and tangible beliefs. Catholics recite their creed at every Mass.

Curia The offices and personnel that assist a bishop govern a diocese. The Roman Curia helps the pope lead the universal church.

deacon An ordained minister with some but not all priestly powers. Transitional deacons plan to become priests and commit to a life of chastity. Married men over 35 may become permanent deacons. They may remarry only with special permission.

diocese An area comprising church properties and institutions run by the local bishop. The Holy See decides what will become a diocese.

ecclesiastical Related to a Christian church or its clergy.

encyclical A letter by the pope to the universal church. These are typically about doctrines, disciplines or morals.

friar From the Latin, "frater," or brother, this title is used by certain religious orders, especially Franciscans and Dominicans. These men may be practicing priests, but not all lead weekly Mass. Unlike other monks, they go out into the world to teach, pray and serve. They take vows of poverty, celibacy and obedience.

Holy See The central government of the Catholic Church, it occupies the Vatican City State. It is treated as a sovereign country.

immaculate conception In Catholic doctrine, Jesus' mother was conceived in the womb of her mother without the original sin that each human carries.

lector Someone who proclaims the readings at Mass.

Lent The 40-day period of fasting and penitence that leads to Easter. Its first day is Ash Wednesday.

monk A man who has taken religious vows, including the vow of poverty, and who isolates from the secular world. Monks vow obedience to their communities, which are called abbeys or priories.

monsignor An honorary title, it recognizes some priests for their function in church governance or for service. In 2014, Pope Francis restricted future designations to diocesan priests over the age of 65.

nuncio A papal ambassador to a civil government.

nuns Women religious whose lives center around prayer and contemplation. They are cloistered apart from public activity. They take solemn vows of poverty, celibacy and obedience. (Please see sisters.)

parish A Catholic parish is a faith community. Parishes are often called the heart of the church. Members might be united by geography, language or ethnicity. Parishes are led by priests operating under the authority of a local bishop.

sisters Women religious who put their prayer into action in a variety of public ministries. These include healthcare, education, social services, guardianship and parish ministry.

synod A collaborative council convened to decide doctrine, administration or application. In the Catholic Church, synods set direction with a series of councils.

Transfiguration This is the event when apostles Peter, James and John went to a mountaintop with Jesus. He was in his divine form and was with the Israelite prophets Moses and Elijah. There, God spoke and Jesus revealed his true nature and foretold his death and resurrection.

transubstantiation The act that believers say changes bread and wine into the body and blood of Christ. Their appearance does not change.

tribunal A judicial person or small group that exercises church decisions in legal matters.

Trinity The representation of God as a unified Father, Son and Holy Spirit. These entities were revealed in succession.

Vatican II The Second Ecumenical Council of the Vatican was only the second such council in almost 100 years. It spanned 1962-1965. Massive changes from Vatican II continue to roll out and generate controversy more than 60 years later.

virgin birth The belief that Jesus was conceived by the Holy Spirit without sexual relations. Not to be confused with the immaculate conception.

Beliefs

1 What do Catholics believe?

Core Roman Catholic beliefs are documented in the creeds, their statements or professions of faith. This is the Nicene Creed, one of the two main versions Catholics use. The other is the Apostles' Creed. The Nicene Creed is accepted by the Roman Catholic, Eastern Orthodox, Anglican and major Protestant churches.

> *I believe in one God,*
>
> *the Father almighty,*
>
> *maker of heaven and earth, of all things visible and invisible.*
>
> *I believe in one Lord Jesus Christ, the Only Begotten Son of God, born of the Father before all ages. God from God, Light from Light, true God from true God, begotten, not made, consubstantial with the Father; through him all things were made. For us men and for our salvation he came down from heaven, and by the Holy Spirit was incarnate of the Virgin Mary and became man. For our sake he was crucified under Pontius Pilate, he suffered death and was buried, and rose again on the third day in accordance with the Scriptures. He*

ascended into heaven and is seated at the right hand of the Father. He will come again in glory to judge the living and the dead, and his kingdom will have no end.

I believe in the Holy Spirit, the Lord, the giver of life, who proceeds from the Father and the Son, who with the Father and the Son is adored and glorified, who has spoken through the prophets.

I believe in one, holy, catholic and apostolic Church. I confess one baptism for the forgiveness of sins and I look forward to the resurrection of the dead and the life of the world to come. Amen.

2 Who do Catholics say God is?

Catholics believe in one God with three persons: the Father, the Son and the Holy Spirit. God the Father is the creator of heaven and Earth. Jesus, the Son of God, is fully divine and fully human. Catholicism teaches that God is the very definition of perfect love: pure, just and all-knowing.

3 Who is the Holy Spirit?

The third entity is the spirit of God and calls people into faith in the Trinity. The Holy Spirit also guides believers. Although revealed last, the Catholic catechism describes the Holy Spirit as the first messenger. It says, "The Holy Spirit is the first to awaken faith in us and to communicate to us the new life, which is to 'know the Father and the one whom he has sent, Jesus Christ.'" The Holy Spirit is God's continuing presence on Earth.

4 Do Catholics believe in heaven and hell?

Catholics believe that after physical death, the soul enters either heaven or hell. Heaven is a state of eternal happiness where those who die in a state of grace are with God for eternity. Hell, for those who die without repenting of their sins and receiving God's mercy, are forever separated from God. The church teaches that no one is predestined for either heaven or hell. Salvation is a gift from God received through the seven sacraments.

5 Do Catholics believe non-members cannot get into heaven?

It is taught that the church is Jesus' path to salvation. Each individual will be judged based on the grace they are given and the way they respond to it. People who are ignorant of the church are not condemned.

6 What is purgatory?

Purgatory is not directly referenced in the Bible, and Catholics differ as to its existence The catechism defines purgatory's role as the "final purification" of souls. In purgatory, souls can achieve the holiness required to enter heaven and be with Christ.

7 Are all sins equally bad?

Sins are categorized. Mortal sins, such as murder, are severe sins in which a person intentionally turns away from God. Venial sins are less severe. Those who repent their sins and take steps to reform can be forgiven. Mortal sins have three elements. They must be serious, done with full knowledge of that seriousness and with full consent of the person's will. If any of these is lacking, the sin is considered venial.

8 What is original sin?

This is the concept that all humans are born with sin. The original sin was Adam and Eve turning from God and listening to Satan. For this, they were ejected from the Garden of Eden. Catholics believe that original sin is passed down through the generations. So, they are baptized to be born again without that sin.

9 Who is the Virgin Mary?

The New Testament and the creeds say Mary is Jesus' mother. The catechism elaborates that, as a virgin, Mary conceived Jesus through the powers of God, not man. "Virgin birth" is different from Mary's "immaculate conception." The second term refers to Mary's nature at the moment she was conceived. In 1854, Pope Pius IX declared that Mary had been conceived and born without original sin.

Sacraments

10 What are sacraments?

Sacraments are signs established by Christ to give grace to humans. Some sacraments are received only once. Others may be celebrated often. It is rare for a person to receive all seven. They are:

Baptism

This is admittance to the Catholic faith. It brings sanctifying grace and is the prerequisite to all other sacraments. It cleanses original sin and any sin someone has committed to that point in their life. Catholics often are baptized during infancy. Older initiates prepare for baptism through the Order of Christian Initiation of Adults. Catholics are baptized only once. Catholics believe one's old self dies, and a new self emerges during baptism. Typically, a priest or deacon will call upon the Holy Trinity and sprinkle or pour holy water on the candidate's head in the presence of godparents or sponsors. The cleric says, "I baptize you in the name of the Father and of the Son and of the Holy Spirit." Full submersion baptism, rooted in the Old Testament, symbolizes arising with Christ. Some other Christian faiths prefer submersion, and candidates wait until they are old enough to decide for themselves to accept Christ. Technically, anyone can baptize, although church law says it should be done by a priest or deacon except for emergencies. Baptism, along with The Eucharist and Confirmation are sacraments of initiation.

Reconciliation

Catholics seek forgiveness for sin by appealing to God through a priest. Also called confession, this requires reflection, taking accountability for one's sins and resolving to change. People express remorse and ask to be brought back into unity with God and the church. The priest, as mediator, may grant an act of penance. This can mean making amends or saying prayers of contrition. The forgiven Catholic strives to cease repeating the sins. Catholics may seek confession weekly, though most do not. More participate before Easter. Catholics should receive the sacrament annually. A 2024 EWTN News/RealClear Opinion Research survey found that 58 percent do. While reconciliation was conceived to be practiced individually, general absolution may be offered in times of crisis. The Vatican reaffirmed this during the COVID-19 pandemic.

The Eucharist

Also called Holy Communion, this is receiving bread and wine that has been transformed into the body and blood of Christ. The consecration and Communion are the most important parts of the Mass service. The sacrament is based on Jesus' words at Passover when he shared bread and wine with his disciples. The apostle Luke wrote that Jesus said, "This is my body given for you; do this in remembrance of me." The name of the sacrament comes from "communion" meaning being in unity with other people and God. The term Eucharist is used by Catholics,

Anglicans, Lutherans, Eastern and Oriental Orthodox and others. Catholics are encouraged to receive Communion frequently. The church teaches that though physical qualities do not change, the bread and wine become Jesus' body and blood. About one-third of U.S. Catholics surveyed in a 2019 Pew Research Center study said they believe this.

Confirmation

This usually is received at or after "the age of discretion." The United States Conference of Catholic Bishops puts this age between 7 and 16. Confirmation makes someone a full member of the church. Candidates choose their own confirmation name. This is usually based on a saint. The names are spiritual and not a legal name change. For adult converts, confirmation occurs immediately after baptism. A priest or a bishop will guide the confirmation process and anoint the person's head with holy oil, called chrism. The person is then "sealed with the gift of the Holy Spirit," who is said to be within that person.

Holy orders

Men are ordained into the priesthood or clerical state in this sacrament. Depending on its degree, ordination conveys the power to consecrate the Eucharist, confirm, anoint, marry couples, forgive sins and, for bishops, ordain others. Ordination takes place during a sacramental Mass. In it, a bishop places his hands on the head of the man being ordained and bestows prayers and blessings. Roman Catholic men who make this sacrament are expected to remain celibate and unmarried. There are degrees of holy orders for deacons, priests and bishops. Holy orders and matrimony are called sacraments of service.

Matrimony

This is the covenant between a husband and wife. Marriage is a sacred and permanent union among God, a man and a woman. Through marriage, a couple reflects Christ's spousal love for the church. In 2021, the Vatican reaffirmed that the church does not condone same-sex marriages, despite increasing social and legal acceptance of them. In 2023, Pope Francis allowed priests to bless same-sex unions, but not same-sex marriages.

Rite of anointing

Also called the anointing of the sick, this is for people experiencing illness or old age. It may be administered even if the person is not near death, as was implied by an older name, "last rites." The sacrament invites the Holy Spirit's gifts of peace and courage. The sacrament asks that, if it is God's will, the person will be healed.

11 What is distinctive about Catholic funerals?

Catholics believe in an afterlife and an immortal soul. The United States Conference of Catholic Bishops stresses "the respect and honor due to the human body." The church allows cremation but asks that it happens after funeral services. Catholic cemeteries have added columbaria to hold cremated remains.

Worship

12 How often do Catholics attend Mass?

In 1970, more than half of America's Catholics said they went to Mass at least once a week on Sunday or late Saturday. By 2022, that had fallen to 17 percent, according to the Center for Applied Research in the Apostolate affiliated with Georgetown University. Among millennials, the number is just 9 percent. The Pew Research Center has higher numbers. Catholics are expected to also attend Mass on Easter, Christmas and five more Holy Days of Obligation. They are:

- Jan. 1: Solemnity of Mary
- 40 days after Easter: feast of Jesus' Ascension into heaven
- Aug. 15: The Assumption of Mary into heaven
- Nov. 1: All Saints' Day
- Dec. 8: Feast of the Immaculate Conception.

13 What do Catholics believe happens during the Eucharist?

The Catholic Church teaches that consecration by a priest changes bread and wine into the literal body and blood of Christ. This change is called transubstantiation. It means that although the bread and wine appear as they did before consecration, their substance has changed. Not all Christian religions believe the bread and wine change substance.

14 Are non-Catholics welcome at Mass?

Guests are welcome. Often, they are greeted publicly at the beginning of the service. Prayer cards or books called missalettes are available in pews to guide people. These contain scripture readings and prayers used throughout the Mass. Attire and practices vary from church to church, but business casual is widely accepted. If you have never been, watch people around you for cues about when to sit, stand and kneel. Online videos of the Mass can give an idea in advance of what to expect.

15 May non-Catholics receive the Eucharist?

Baptism and confession are prerequisites to receiving this sacrament. The United States Conference of Catholic Bishops says "members of those churches with whom we are not yet fully united are ordinarily not admitted to Holy Communion." At Communion, non-Catholics may remain seated or join the line. Rather than receive the Eucharist, they cross their arms across their chest to receive a blessing.

16 When do Catholics pray?

In addition to Mass, some Catholics pray throughout the day, such as upon rising, meals and bedtime. Many pray spontaneously. Catholics use scripted prayers, such as "The Hail Mary," or improvise. In Pew Research's 2014 religious landscapes survey, 60.2 percent of Catholics said they pray at least once a day.

17 What does making the sign of the cross mean?

This action has moved over even to non-religious settings. It is seen at sporting events, in pop culture and movies. To Catholics, making the sign of the cross is a physical and verbal reminder of a commitment to God. The sign is made by raising the fingers of the right hand to the head ("In the name of the Father"), midsection ("and the Son"), left shoulder ("and the Holy Spirit") and right shoulder ("Amen"). Catholics also use their right thumb to sign a cross on their forehead, lips and chest before the Gospel is read during Mass. This signifies that the words will direct thoughts, words and deeds. Priests may sign a cross in the air as a blessing. Incense burners, called censers, may be swung in the pattern of a cross. People also trace the sign on children's foreheads as a blessing.

18 What is the significance of priests' robes?

Priests put on vestments for Mass in a specific order with prayers asking God to purify, protect and bless him. The color of the outer vestment reflects the season in the church calendar. Green, used for most of the year, symbolizes hope. Red is for blood. At Easter and Christmas, white signifies rejoicing. Gold means light. Black is for mourning. For Lent and Advent, purple reflects sorrow and suffering, while pink symbolizes joy.

19 What does it mean to be excommunicated?

Catholics can be excommunicated for what are considered to be grave transgressions of church teachings. It can also happen to clerics who operate outside their authority. Excommunication bars Catholics from receiving Communion and clergy from ministering. Excommunication is typically a rare last resort that follows attempts at negotiation and reconciliation. It is intended to be temporary encouragement to repent so people will return. Excommunicated people remain Catholics and may attend Mass. Excommunication can be lifted by the pope or a bishop.

Practices

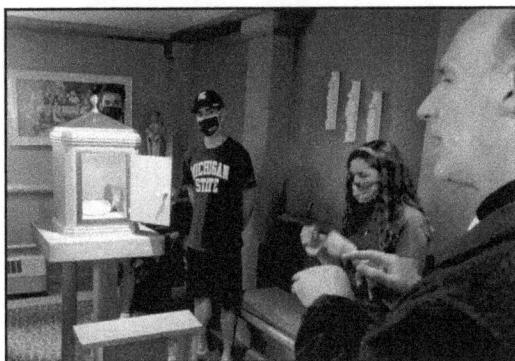

Father Gordon Reigle shows
student authors of this guide the
tabernacle at St. John Church.

20 What are the characteristics of church architecture?

Historically, the most formal Catholic architecture had a
floorplan in the shape of a cross. Catholic churches come
in many styles today but share important interior elements.
There is an altar where the priest says Mass. Seating,
usually in pews, faces the altar from its front and sides.
There is a crucifix, which is a cross bearing a representation
of Christ before or after his death. Some display a risen
Christ. There will also be a tabernacle. The word means
"dwelling" for God's home on Earth. It is typically an
ornamented, locking box. It houses the consecrated
Eucharist. A burning light or candle in a red glass signifies
that the blessed sacrament is present in that tabernacle.
There will be a baptismal font in the church. It generally

contains blessed holy water which people may use to sign themselves with the cross. Some Catholic churches have a small pool for baptismal immersions.

21 Why do churches have religious art and stained glass?

Statues and paintings of saints direct thoughts toward Christian qualities. People find inspiration and role models in the people and stories depicted in the artwork. Statues and paintings of saints have been misinterpreted as idol worship. That is not what is going on. Visualizations are not worshiped but can foster contemplation and prayer. Stained glass windows allow natural and colored light into churches, temples and other religious buildings and set a mood. Stained glass goes back to the seventh century, C.E. They reached their zenith in 1100-1500 C.E. In those days, when books were scarce and most people could not read, windows told stories.

22 What is the rosary?

This term refers to a set of prayers and to the string of 59 beads, crucifix and medal used to keep track of the prayers. The rosary begins with the "Apostles' Creed." Then five decades, or sets of 10, "Hail Mary" prayers are said. Between the decades, there is a larger bead where one prays the "Our Father," and a short prayer, the "Glory Be." The rosary ends with the "Hail, Holy Queen." There are 20 mysteries, with the decades accounting for each of four categories. They are the Glorious Mysteries, the Joyful Mysteries, the Sorrowful Mysteries and the Luminous

Mysteries. Each reflects on events of Christ's life from scripture. The rosary can be prayed privately or in a group, silently or aloud, all at once or over days. It is OK to wear a rosary as a sign of faith or a reminder to pray. The church discourages wearing rosaries as fashion accessories. Praying with beads goes back centuries in many faith groups. The church attributes the specific form of the rosary to a vision experienced by St. Dominic in 1214.

23 What are the major holidays in the Catholic calendar?

The pinnacle of the Catholic calendar is Easter Sunday, commemorating Jesus' resurrection. The date follows a lunar pattern. Christmas is next most important in the Catholic Church and is always on Dec. 25. Then there are Holy Days of Obligation and solemn holy days. For these, attendance at Mass is recommended but not required. Important holy days in Lent are Ash Wednesday at the beginning and Good Friday, two days before Easter. These are days of abstinence and fasting, as are other Fridays in Lent.

24 What does Ash Wednesday signify?

This Day of Ashes symbolizes repentance. A cross of ashes is marked on the believer's forehead while the administrator of the ashes says, "Remember that you are dust, and to dust you shall return," or "Repent and believe in the Gospel." The ashes are made by burning palm branches from the preceding year's Palm Sunday, the one before Easter. On that day, worshippers use palm branches to commemorate Jesus' ride into Jerusalem. On Ash Wednesday, many wear ashes the rest of the day, but there is no rule about this. Several denominations observe Ash Wednesday. Mass attendance on that day is not required.

25 What are the stations of the cross?

The stations of the cross are 14 plaques, statues or other depictions adorned with a cross of moments from when Jesus was sentenced to die through his crucifixion and burial. The stations may be inside a church or outdoors. They begin with Jesus being condemned by Pontius Pilate. They end with Jesus being laid in the tomb. Especially during Lent, Catholics are encouraged to make the stations of the cross. At each station, Catholics pray and contemplate what Jesus endured in his humiliating ordeal, which is called "the passion."

"Jesus falls for the second time," the sixth of the 14 stations of the cross. This is in Detroit's Ste. Anne's Catholic Church, home of the second oldest Catholic parish in the United States, founded in 1701.

Identity

26 How is Catholicism different from other Christian religions?

There are many differences among Orthodoxy, Protestantism and Roman Catholicism.

Orthodox Christians believe salvation is a life-long process of faith working through love. They believe tradition is the only source of divine revelation. Catholic and Orthodox Christians are taught that consecration transforms bread and wine into the body and blood of Christ. Eastern Orthodox and Roman Catholics favor infant baptism.

Protestants believe salvation is a gift from God given by Jesus and obtained by faith in Christ alone. Protestantism was founded on the idea that scripture is the guide. Protestants see the Eucharist as a symbol that commemorates what Christ sacrificed; the Eucharist does not change substance. Protestants favor adult baptism.

Catholics believe the sacraments lead to salvation. All salvation is through Jesus Christ. Catholics also believe in sacred scripture and sacred tradition. Roman Catholics favor infant baptism, except in the case of conversions. Some U.S. Catholic parishes have been moving from sprinkling to immersion baptisms, though both are allowed. Catholics consider seven books — known as the

Deuterocanon, or Apocrypha to Protestants — to be part of the Bible. Protestants do not.

Other Christ-centered religions, such as Anabaptism, Christian Science and the Church of Jesus Christ of Latter-day Saints, use additional texts and have different beliefs about the nature of God and practices.

27 Who are saints?

To Catholics, saints are examples of how to follow Christ. Catholics venerate saints but should not worship them. Rather, Catholics look to saints for guidance and ask them to intercede on their behalf. Appealing to saints is like asking someone to pray for you. Some Catholics implore saints based on what they are known for. Based on their lives, some saints are declared patrons of qualities or locations. A common subject of appeals for help finding misplaced items is St. Anthony, patron saint of lost things. This followed an incident in which Anthony's book of psalms disappeared. He prayed for its recovery and the novice who had taken it returned it. Churches named for a saint might celebrate that saint's feast day.

28 How is sainthood decided?

The Catholic Church specifies that everyone in heaven, known or unknown, is a saint. Official, verified sainthood, on the other hand, comes from a process called canonization. It can take many years and several steps. Investigation takes years. It begins after the candidate has been deceased for five years and a local petition is written. A report must be approved by a succession of panels including a tribunal, nine theologians and the Congregation for the Causes of Saints, composed of cardinals and bishops. Finally, there must be proof of two miracles arising from the candidate's intercession. The pope, who has seen the interim reports, canonizes the saint.

29 What is a "cafeteria Catholic"?

This term arose in the 1980s to describe progressive Catholics who follow some doctrines but not others. They might follow teachings on poverty and peace but not birth control, abortion, divorce or same-sex relationships. It is a derogatory term.

30 What is a "cradle Catholic"?

"Cradle Catholics" have been church members since birth. They did not convert or choose to be baptized. Their implicit challenge is to live their faith with passion and not practice out of habit alone.

Milestones

31 When did the Catholic Church begin?

All Christian churches trace roots to the teachings of Jesus Christ in Judea, in what is now the Palestinian territories. The Catholic Church teaches that Jesus died in 33 C.E. The Roman Empire banned Christianity for 280 years. The church began to expand after the ban was lifted in 325 C.E.

32 What was Vatican II?

Catholic leaders from around the world were summoned to the Vatican by Pope John XXIII. They met annually in 1962-1965. John XXIII died in 1963 and was succeeded by Pope Paul VI. At the onset, John stated three goals: to promote Catholic truth, to seek unity among Christians and to update Catholic practice. The work by an estimated 2,000 bishops, priests, sisters and laypeople led to massive changes. Churches and the liturgy were redesigned to turn priests around to face congregants. Local languages replaced Latin. The church at large turned toward non-Catholic and non-Christian religions. Lay people had more say running parishes and churches. Sisters were no longer required to adopt religious names. Sisters were encouraged to return to their founding documents, reexamine their mission and determine if a habit suited their work. Each congregation made its own choice. Some made it gradually by going into modified habits. Others made the choice to come out of the habits right away. Sixty years later, the changes are ongoing and still generating controversy. In 2021, Pope Francis discouraged efforts to return the Mass to Latin and issued corrections to Catholics who rejected reforms of the Second Vatican Council. The National Catholic Reporter wrote in 2022 that Pope Francis said in an interview that U.S. "restorers" were trying to gag Vatican II reforms. The news outlet reported that 2023 "was a particularly tumultuous year in the continuing debate over the proper interpretation of the Council."

33 Did U.S. Catholics support the pope?

A 2024 Pew report said three-quarters of Catholics had a positive view of Pope Francis. That was down a little from the 80 percent favorability rating he had been getting since he became pope in 2013. The survey showed Catholic Democrats were much more likely (89 percent) than Catholic Republicans (63 percent) to rate him favorably.

Hierarchy

34 What is the church hierarchy?

Leadership, which is all male, has roughly six levels:
Deacons, the first level, are ordained, like priests and
bishops. they may proclaim the Gospel, preach, baptize,
lead prayers and officiate at marriages and funerals. Those
on their way to the priesthood are transitional deacons
and do not marry. Permanent deacons are not on the path
to become priests. A married man over 35 may become a
permanent deacon. If his wife dies, he needs permission to
remarry.

Priests may be diocesan or religious. Diocesan priests,
about two thirds of the total, lead parishes and report
to the local bishop. Religious priests take an oath to a
religious order but are under the jurisdiction of the local
bishop in their work in any diocese.

Bishops must be 35 or older, with experience in the
priesthood and an advanced degree in theology or canon
law. They lead their diocese, which encompasses the
parishes in their region. There are about 5,500 bishops
worldwide.

Archbishops are considered the "first among equals" of
the bishops in their region. The Catholic Conference of
Ohio, for example, includes the Archdiocese of Cincinnati
and five smaller dioceses. A bishop is sovereign in his

own diocese, and ultimately reports only to the pope. An archbishop has limited privileges related to bishops in his region. Responsibilities include calling regional councils and adjudicating disputes among bishops.

Cardinals are bishops or priests whom the pope appoints to the College of Cardinals. They help govern the church. Their weightiest responsibility is deciding who will be pope. There were 252 cardinals in 2025. Only those under the age of 80 may vote for a pope. In December 2024, 21 appointments by Pope Francis pushed the number of voting cardinals to 140, beyond the often surpassed limit of 120. Voting cardinals in 2023 included 53 from Europe; 24 from Latin America; 22 from Asia; 19 from Africa; 15 from North America; and three from Oceania.

The **pope** leads the church from Vatican City, a city-state surrounded by Rome, Italy. Pope Leo XIV became the 266th successor to Jesus' choice, St. Peter.

Despite their exclusion from church hierarchy, women religious have done and still do much of its work in the United States. They manage and run parishes. They have had leadership roles in building national networks of schools and in healthcare. Orders of brothers, friars and monks also do specialized work, although they are not in the hierarchy, either. Dominicans, who have male and female members as well as a lay branch, pursue truth through holistic education. Franciscan priests and brothers, collectively called friars, were founded by St. Francis of Assisi in the 13th century. They live in communities as he did. A Franciscan offshoot, the Capuchins, emerged in 1525 to revive St. Francis' stricter observances.

35 What are the steps to becoming a priest?

The first step can start in childhood when a boy believes he has a calling to the priesthood. He might have an idea about the type of priesthood he would like. He must pass psychological exams and background checks before entering the seminary. This can happen as early as right after high school. Seminary training could last 5-12 years. The candidate is then ordained as a deacon and later as a priest.

36 Why is there a priest shortage?

The Vatican reported in 2015 that "the number of priests and ordained leaders has dropped significantly, especially in Europe and America." The shortage is measured in raw numbers and in terms of the ratio of Catholics per priest. The National Catholic Reporter attributed the decline to factors including secularization of society, sexual and money scandals and reduced financial support. Celibacy and the long training period have also been cited. Aging also plays a role. U.S. bishops estimated that by 2025, religious sisters, brothers and priests over 70 would outnumber those under age 70 by nearly 4-1. A 2023 survey of more than 3,500 priests by The Catholic Project at Catholic University said young priests, driven by liberal politics and progressive theology, have "all but vanished."

37 Can Catholic clergy get married?

Roman Catholic priests must remain celibate. There are married priests in some Eastern Catholic rites. An ordained priest or deacon generally cannot get married and remain a priest. In special cases, such as if a married Anglican or Lutheran priest becomes Catholic, he may, with permission, become a Catholic priest.

38 Would ending celibacy ease the priest shortage?

In 2022, some European bishops said celibacy is not intrinsic to the priesthood. The early church allowed priests to marry. Pope Francis said, "Celibacy is a gift that the Latin Church preserves, yet it is a gift that, to be lived as a means of sanctification, calls for healthy relationships." In 2024, Archbishop Charles Scicluna, an adviser to Pope Francis, said: "If it were up to me, I would revise the requirement that priests have to be celibate. Experience has shown me that this is something we need to seriously think about." He acknowledged the idea would have strong opposition.

39 How does a man become a monk?

First is the exploration stage, which includes visits to a monastery. The second stage is called a postulancy. That means living in the monastery for six months. The third stage is novitiate, which means growing spiritually. After three or more years of this are simple vows. This is a time of temporary but serious commitment. Monks live in communities, their missions decided by that community or their religious order. Many teach. Some pray and do other work to support themselves. The concluding stage is sacred vows, in which one consecrates his life to God.

The Pope

40 Who elects the pope?

Popes choose the cardinals, who will later elect his successor. In September 2023, Pope Francis named 21 new cardinals. In October 2024, he named 21 more. This significantly raised the percentage of Francis-chosen cardinals who would elect his successor. He named about three quarters of voting-eligible cardinals. According to the Reuters news service, his strategy "increases but does not guarantee — the possibility that the next pope will share his vision of a more progressive, inclusive Church." Pope Francis also made the College of Cardinals more global. Francis himself was the first non-European pope in 1,300 years. The number of cardinals from Europe has declined. The college has more Asian and African members than ever. He named cardinals from the United States, France, Italy, Argentina, Switzerland, South Africa, Spain, Colombia, Hong Kong, Poland, Tanzania, Venezuela, Portugal, Canada, Iran, Serbia, Australia, the second ever from Malaysia and the first from South Sudan.

41 How do the cardinals vote?

To elect a pope, cardinal electors gather at the Vatican for secret meetings called conclaves. There are as many as four votes per day until someone receives two-thirds of the vote. Since 1379, every pope has come from the College of Cardinals, though this is not required. After a vote, cardinals signal their decision by releasing smoke through a chimney on the Sistine Chapel. Black smoke means the electors do not have a decision. When two-thirds agree, they release white smoke, and the bells of St. Peter's Basilica ring.

42 Is the pope infallible?

The dogma of infallibility goes back to 1870. It is rarely applied. First, infallibility covers only statements about doctrine on faith or morals. Second, the statement must be made to the global church. Third, the pontiff must be speaking ex cathedra — "from the chair" of St. Peter, whom Jesus chose to lead the church. In these cases, the church teaches that the Holy Spirit will save the pope from speaking incorrectly.

43 Are popes elected for life?

Popes typically hold office for life. The average tenure is seven years. In 2013, Pope Benedict XVI became the first pope in 600 years to resign, and Francis was elected. Benedict lived for almost 10 more years until Dec. 31, 2022. Having Francis, a progressive pope, follow a retired traditionalist divided allegiances. Shortly before his death on April 21, 2025, it was revealed the pope had signed a resignation letter shortly after his installation to be used if he became incapacitated.

44 Must Catholics obey the pope?

The pope's realm is religious, not governmental or judicial. However, many social issues have religious implications. Some popes have engaged social issues such as peace, climate change, racial or economic equity and abortion. Others have not. Popes have no direct authority to change laws or policies but may try to influence them.

Women in the Church

45 Why can't women be priests?

Church doctrine says priests represent the likeness of Jesus. Pope John Paul II wrote that priesthood is reserved for men because Christ chose only men as apostles.

46 What roles do women serve in the church?

The primary official roles are as sisters and nuns. The first Catholic women religious came to the United States in 1727. They ran the nation's largest private school system and started hundreds of nonprofit hospitals. They provided medical care to Civil War soldiers, survivors of the Titanic sinking and after 9/11. There are thousands of women in hundreds of Catholic orders, serving communities in many capacities. Lutherans, Anglicans, Orthodox Christians and various streams of Buddhism also have nuns or sisters.

47 Are sisters and nuns the same?

No. Nuns lead lives of contemplation and prayer. They are cloistered apart from public activity. Sisters work in health care, education and parish ministry. They are also lawyers, authors, podcast hosts, social workers, therapists, chefs, spiritual directors, non-profit managers and humanitarian aid workers. Nuns and sisters are all women religious and may be addressed as "sister." The distinction is blurred by casual language and pop culture productions such as "Nunsense" and "Sister Act." Women religious appreciate it when people pay attention to whether they are a nun or a sister. America magazine, a Jesuit ministry, reported in 2021 that a survey found religious sisters and nuns to be the most trusted group of Catholic leaders. The survey was conducted with Georgetown University's Center for Applied Research of the Apostolate. In addition to women religious, lay women are a pillar of the church. They assist at Mass, raise funds, organize events such as prayer groups, Bible studies and justice ministries. They lead retreats and outreach projects. U.S. religion scholar Catherine Lowman Wessinger estimates that women hold 85 percent of church roles that do not require ordination.

48 What is the process for becoming a sister or nun?

Orders have different processes and terminology but are generally similar. Some orders require college degrees and psychological testing. The process for the Sisters of Mercy, the largest order in the United States, has eight stages. The process takes at least seven years.

Inquiry: Guidance about the call from a vocation minister, a retreat, serving the needs of the community

Application: Retreats, live-in experiences, meetings with a spiritual director and other sisters, ministry visits

Pre-candidacy: Getting to know the community

Welcoming ceremony: A ritual celebration of prayer for the new candidate

Candidacy: A year focused on the transition to religious life plus a year focused on ministry, studying theology, and preparation

Novitiate phase: A year of intense reflection and an apostolic year of ministerial activity

Temporary profession: Three to six years for the first profession of vows, ministry or studies while living within the community

Full profession: Final vows of poverty, celibacy, obedience and service

49 Do women religious still wear habits?

Some do, but this has become less common. Three events beginning in the 1950s led to a decline in habit-wearing. In the 1950s, Pope Pius XII suggested that women religious dress more like the people in the communities they served. In 1962, Vatican II began its push to make the church, including dress, more compatible with the current needs of ministry and community. In 1963, Betty Freidan's "The Feminine Mystique" helped launch the Women's Movement. Most women religious do not wear habits, although some orders and some individuals choose to. Some wear habits as a sign of their calling to Christ. Others wear them to signify their area of service, such as a sister working in a hospital.

50 What are the origins of habits?

Habits go back centuries to medieval times. Some women wore them as a sign of their consecration to God. Others wore habits to blend in with their communities. A full habit may include:

Tunic: A loose, full-length garment. Colors vary by religious order, and some are trimmed with a second color. Some have been made of coarse cloth to symbolize the vow of poverty.

Scapular: A symbolic front-and-back apron.

Cincture: A leather, wool or lanyard belt.

Coif: The headpiece typically has a white cap and a wimple that may cover the neck or the neck and cheeks. Head coverings vary.

Veil: If worn, this is pinned over the coif.

Some orders also wear rosaries. Habits may be as simple as a dress and veil.

51 Is there a shortage of women religious?

The decline in the numbers of women religious, who do much of the Catholic Church's work, is steeper than the decline in priests. In 2022, Georgetown's Center for Applied Research in the Apostolate reported there were fewer than 42,000 sisters in America, a 76 percent decline over 50 years. The decline is accelerating. The center

Nuns have declined faster than priests in U.S.

Religious sisters in the United States do a lot of work in churches and schools and outnumber priests. However, the number of U.S. nuns has declined faster than the number of priests since 1965.

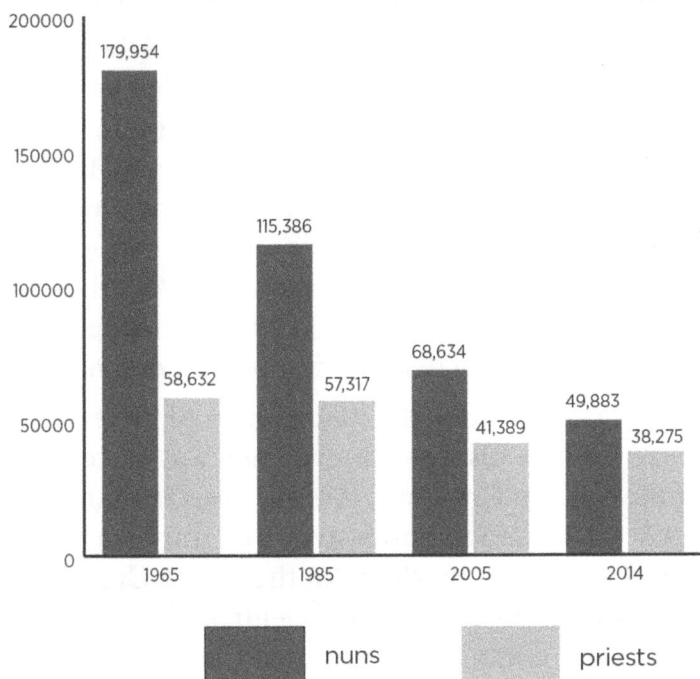

Source: Center for Applied Research in the Apostolate, Georgetown University.
Graphic by Claire Heise

reported a 72 percent drop from 180,000 to 50,000 in the 50 years from 1965 to 2014. Aging appears to be one factor. In 2009, the center said there were more sisters over the age of 90 than under the age of 60. At the rate sisters are disappearing, it was estimated there will be fewer than 1,000 U.S. women religious by 2042. While the number of priests also has fallen, it has done so at a much slower rate, about 35 percent. Sisters, who used to outnumber priests about 3:1, will soon be outnumbered by priests. Around the world, vocations are up for priests, down for women religious.

52 Are new roles opening for women?

In 2016, Pope Francis created a commission of bishops to study whether to ordain women deacons. It failed to reach a conclusion. So, he created a second commission in 2020. It was also inconclusive. In May 2024, several issues that had been scheduled for a global synod discussion were tabled. They included women deacons and ordination, celibacy and broader LGBTQ+ inclusion. That October, bishops announced female ordination will not happen for now. This dashed almost a decade of hope by women.

In 2022, the pope appointed the first women to review candidates to become bishops. One woman was secretary general of the Vatican City State. Another was the former superior general of the Salesian Sisters. The third was a consecrated virgin and president of the World Union of Catholic Women's Organizations. Heidi Schlumpf, formerly executive editor of the National Catholic Reporter, wrote that the reactions of U.S. Catholic women to these appointments were mixed. The Women's Ordination Conference noted "deep irony that women may now aid in selecting bishops, a role they themselves are prohibited from holding on account of their gender." In 2025, Francis appointed the first woman to reach the top position in an office of the Holy See. Sister Simona Brambilla will oversee the world's Catholic religious orders and congregations.

53 Who are consecrated virgins?

This is a lesser known calling for women religious. They dedicate their virginity to God and belong to Christ in the Catholic Church. They do not marry. They do not join orders or go through the formation steps of sisters and nuns. They can work outside the church.

54 May women and girls be altar servers?

While local bishops have been letting women and girls help at the Mass for many years, the church did not formalize this until 2021. Pope Francis expanded church law to formally authorize women to do more during Mass. This allowed them to be lectors, assist priests on the altar and administer the Eucharist.

55 Why do some women wear veils in church?

Chapel veils, also called mantillas, are usually circular or triangular pieces of lace that cover a woman's head. Veils symbolize modesty and humility before God and have biblical origins. Before the Second Vatican Council, women were required to cover their heads at Mass. Now, head coverings for women are optional and far less common. Wearing a veil today can have a multitude of meanings including political ones. It is best to not assume why a woman is wearing one. Ask her.

Myths & Stereotypes

56 Are Catholics Christian?

Catholics dedicate their spiritual lives to following Jesus Christ and his teachings. Some Christian denominations disagree with Catholics about theology and practice. Denominations have many different ways of following Christ and some say others are doing it wrong.

57 Do Catholics worship Mary?

No. The church says Mary holds an exalted place because of her role as the mother of Jesus. Three of the church's five Holy Days of Obligation center on Mary. Catholics pray to her to intercede for them. But she is not God, and she is not divine. Very little about her life is known, and teachings from her have not been passed down in scriptures. The best way to describe Catholic attitudes about Mary is to say that she is venerated or revered.

58 Do Catholics believe in limbo?

For centuries, Catholic teaching maintained there must be a place for unbaptized babies who died and for good people who lived before the time of Christ. However, limbo was never part of church doctrine. Church leaders began to question the concept. In his days as a cardinal, Pope Benedict XVI wrote that limbo was "only a theological hypothesis ... never a defined truth of faith." In 1992, The "Catechism of the Catholic Church" dropped its mention of limbo. In a 2007 document, Benedict XVI ended the matter. A New York Times headline joked "Pope Closes Limbo."

59 Do Catholics practice exorcism?

The United States Conference of Catholic Bishops treats exorcisms as healings. It has a long protocol for using prayer against the power of the devil in a person or place. Exorcisms are not like their movie portrayals. There are minor exorcisms for those preparing for conversion or baptism. A major exorcism for possession can be performed only by a bishop or by a priest with approval.

60 Do Catholics believe in conventional medicine?

The church runs the largest group of nonprofit health-care providers in the country, according to the Catholic Health Association of the United States. It claims "More than 600 hospitals and 1,600 long-term care and other health facilities in all 50 states." They have cared for more than one in seven medical patients in the country. Questions about church support for conventional medicine could arise from the church's history of healing miracles. Opposition to abortion may be another factor.

Demographics

61 How large is the U.S. Catholic Church?

The Pew Research Center estimates that 52 million U.S. adults identify as Catholics. That is 20 percent of the adult population. The percentage has remained there since 2014 but is less than the 24 percent reported for 2007. The U.S. has more Catholics than all but three other countries, according to the Vatican's statistical yearbook. Those countries are Brazil, Mexico and the Philippines.

62 Where are the largest percentages of U.S. Catholics?

Clifford Grammich, a political scientist who worked on the U.S. Religion Census, told the Catholic News Agency that the population is shifting. He said, "50 years ago, 71 percent of U.S. Catholics were in the Northeast and Midwest." That share declined to 45 percent in 2020. He said the South has more Catholics than any other region and that there are more Catholics than Southern Baptists in Missouri and Virginia.

Hispanic Catholics & White Catholics

Percent of Americans who are Hispanic Catholics vs. percent who are White Catholics

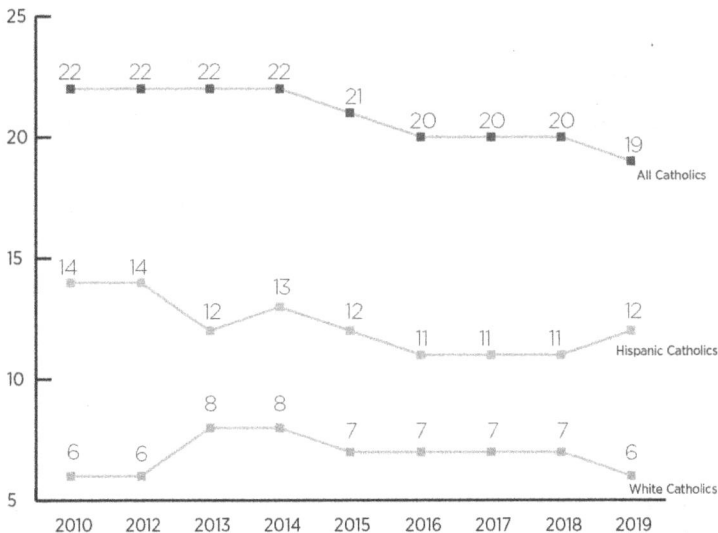

	2010	2012	2013	2014	2015	2016	2017	2018	2019
All Catholics	22	22	22	22	21	20	20	20	19
Hispanic Catholics	14	14	12	13	12	11	11	11	12
White Catholics	6	6	8	8	7	7	7	7	6

Source: PRRI Surveys, 2010-2019   Graphic by Katie Reichel

63 What is the ethnic or racial makeup of U.S. Catholics?

The largest groups of U.S. Catholics are White at 57 percent and Hispanic/Latino at 33 percent. The rest of U.S. Catholics identify as Asian, 4 percent; Black, 2 percent; and other races, 3 percent. Non-Hispanic White Catholics have decreased by 8 percentage points since 2007. Hispanics have risen by 4 percentage points. According to Pew, Catholics have higher Hispanic and immigrant representation than most other religions in the United States. Ethnicity varies by region. In 2023, an estimated 80 percent of Catholics in the Midwest were White and an estimated 17 percent were Hispanic. In the West, Hispanic

Catholics numbered 55 percent while White Catholics were 30 percent. In the Northeast, 72 percent of Catholics were White and 19 percent were Hispanic.

64 Is the Catholic population aging?

The average age of U.S. Catholics is rising faster than the average for the U.S. population overall. According to a 2024 Pew report, 58 percent of Catholic adults are 50 or older. Among all adults in the survey, 48 percent were in that bracket. Hispanic Catholics bring the average age of Catholics younger. Forty-three percent of Hispanic Catholics are 50 or older, while 68 percent of White Catholics are 50 or older.

65 Do Catholics evangelize?

The Catholic Church has pursued conversions for centuries. It actively sought converts in North America and has missions around the world today. Recently, the church has focused on introducing the Gospel to people that are questioning their faith. This new evangelization was promoted by Pope John Paul II. He wanted to reach former Catholics and people never exposed to the Gospel. Today, efforts are aimed at more respectfully reaching out to Protestants and former Catholics who are now religiously unaffiliated. Pope Francis said, "Evangelizing is not about filling an empty container; it is ultimately about bringing to light what God has already begun to accomplish."

Families

66 May non-Catholics get married in the church?

Religiously mixed marriages are allowed with conditions. The Catholic may be asked to pledge to stay in the church. Their spouse may be asked to allow children to be raised Catholic. There are instances where the bishop can decline the use of a church by a person judged to be "hostile" toward Catholicism. Other religions' clergy may lead a part of the ceremony, but may not officiate. A 2014 Pew survey stated that about 25 percent of U.S. Catholics marry non-Catholics.

67 May Catholics divorce and remarry?

Catholics may get remarried within the church after a divorce if the previous marriage has been annulled. The church says Catholics who have remarried without an annulment are not eligible to receive Communion. A Pew survey found roughly 25 percent of U.S. Catholics have had a divorce. Nine percent have remarried. A quarter of divorced Catholics have sought annulments.

68 What is an annulment?

An annulment is a declaration by the church that the marriage was never valid. The church cites "very well-defined canonical grounds" for annulments. It lists 20. Some are: mental illness, psychological disorder, fraud, marriage by force or fear and denial of the religious importance of Catholic marriage.

69 What size are Catholic families?

A Gallup poll released in 2015 found that the average number of children born to Catholics aged 40-59 was 2.3. For comparison, the national average for all people in that age group was 2.1 children. Family size for Catholics is going down, according to the University of Chicago's General Social Survey. It reported the median number of children for Baby Boomers and Gen X Catholics, born from 1943 to 1980, was two. The average for older Catholics was three.

70 What do Catholics see as the roles of parents?

According to Pew, 90 percent of Catholics said the ideal home for raising children is led by a married mother and father. However, Catholics agreed that single parents, divorced parents, unmarried couples or gay parents are also safe for children. The church teaches parents to share responsibility for raising children in the faith. It does not set gender roles.

Love & Sex

71 How does the church view premarital sex?

The church teaches that God intended sex as a special, loving bond between a married man and woman for uniting the spouses and for procreation. It regards premarital sex as a sin. However, 74 percent of Catholics in a Pew study said premarital sex is OK for couples in committed relationships.

72 What is the church's position on birth control?

The church says couples may naturally plan for children by abstaining from sex when a woman is at the highest probability of becoming pregnant. Artificial contraception is sinful, even within marriage. That is because one of the main purposes of sex is to create. According to a 2016 Pew survey, 13 percent of Catholics believe using artificial birth control is wrong.

Most Catholics say Roe v. Wade should not be overturned

Would you like to see the Supreme Court completely overturn the Roe v. Wade decision or not?

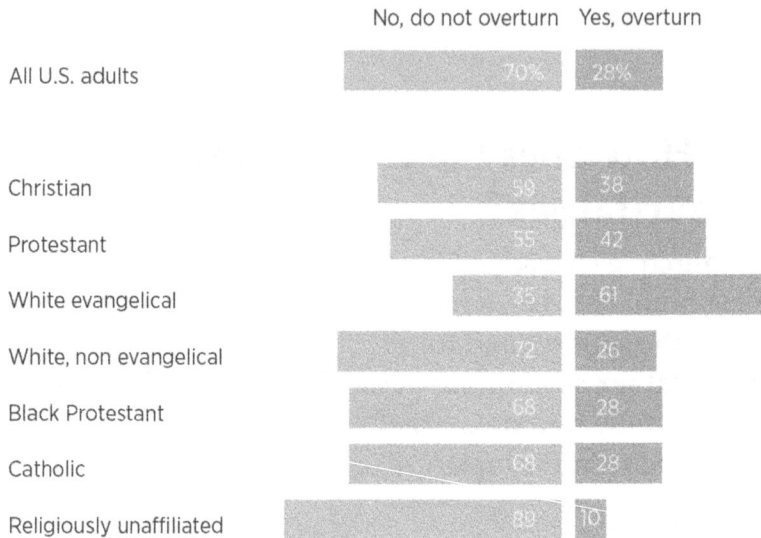

	No, do not overturn	Yes, overturn
All U.S. adults	70%	28%
Christian	59	38
Protestant	55	42
White evangelical	35	61
White, non evangelical	72	26
Black Protestant	68	28
Catholic	68	28
Religiously unaffiliated	89	10

Source: Pew Research Center   Graphic by Vidalia Wenzlick

73 What are Catholics' views on abortion?

The church teaches that life begins at conception, and abortion is immoral because it is taking a life. Many Catholics actively campaign against abortion. However, a May 2022 Associated Press-NORC Center for Public Affairs Research poll found that 63 percent of Catholic adults said abortion should be legal in all or most cases. Sixty-eight percent supported Roe v. Wade. It was overturned the month after the survey. Pew Research found feelings regarding abortion have a political side.

More than half of U.S. Catholics favor legalized abortion

% who say abortion should be...

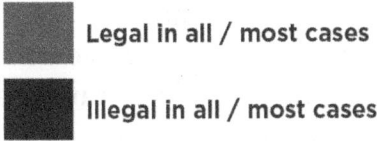

■ **Legal in all / most cases**

■ **Illegal in all / most cases**

* type of Protestant

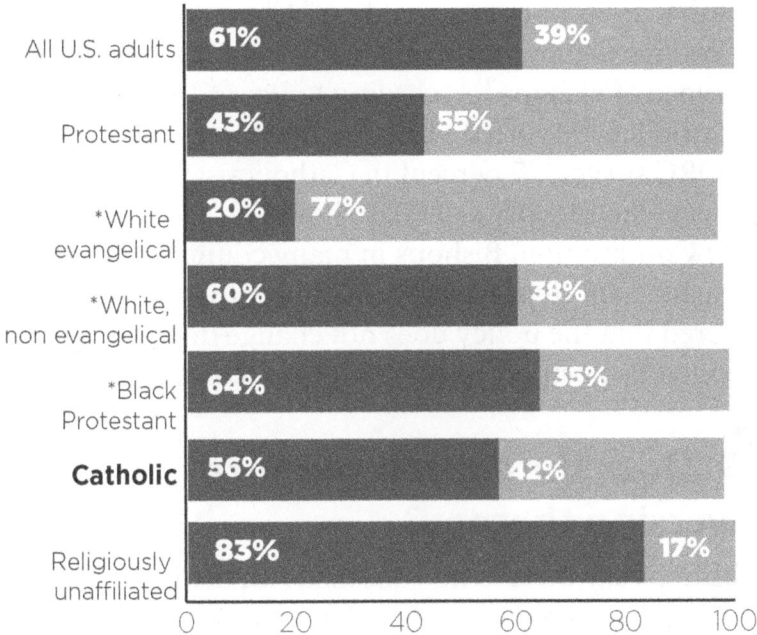

Group	Legal	Illegal
All U.S. adults	61%	39%
Protestant	43%	55%
*White evangelical	20%	77%
*White, non evangelical	60%	38%
*Black Protestant	64%	35%
Catholic	56%	42%
Religiously unaffiliated	83%	17%

Source: Pew Research Center   Graphic by Sydney Bowler

Among Catholic Democrats, 78 percent said abortion should be legal in most or all cases. For Catholic Republicans, 43 percent agreed.

74 How does the church regard LGBTQ+ Catholics?

Late in 2023, the Vatican issued what the National Catholic Reporter called a "major doctrinal shift." This was the decision that Catholic priests may bless those involved in same-sex unions and those for divorced people who remarry. The blessings may not be part of a sacramental wedding. The conditions are that the blessings not be part of a liturgy and occur without "clothing, gestures or words that are proper to a wedding." Clergy may proclaim the blessings without texts or rituals from "a national conference of bishops." According to Pew, 61 percent of U.S. Catholics supported same-sex marriage. In the 2022 AP-NORC survey, 77 percent of Catholics said church members who identify as LGBT should be allowed to receive Communion. Bishops in many countries pushed back against approval of the limited blessings. The Vatican countered that the policy does not change doctrine and reaffirmed its position on marriage and sexuality.

75 Does the church support conversion therapy?

U.S. bishops say there is no consensus on the issue. This therapy seeks to change a person's sexual orientation, gender identity or gender expression. It is typically used to change LGBTQ+ people. Pope Francis expressed concern about the interventions. The American Academy of Child and Adolescent Psychiatry says they can be harmful. U.S. bishops advise anyone interested in therapy to see a psychological professional who "understands and supports the church's teaching on homosexuality."

Education

76 What are the educational levels of U.S. Catholics?

The average educational level for Catholics is close to that for all U.S. adults. Pew found that 27 percent of all U.S. adults have college degrees. Twenty-six percent of Catholic adults do. Thirty-two percent of all U.S. adults and 27 percent of Catholic adults have some college but not a degree. Thirty-one percent of both groups said high school was their highest level of education.

77 How many Catholic schools are there?

Catholic schools are the largest and oldest private education network in the country, according to the U.S. bishops. The first U.S. Catholic school opened in St. Augustine, Florida, in 1606. As nativism in the country targeted Catholic immigrants, the church opened many schools. At the beginning of the 20th century, from 1900 to 1920, the number of Catholic elementary schools in the United States grew from an estimated 3,500 to 6,551. Enrollment grew to 1.76 million students. Catholic high schools jumped from about 100 to 1,500 during those years. However, at the end of the century there was a big

Religious affiliations in private schools

Number and percentage of private school students enrolled in pre-kindergarten through grade 12 for each affiliation of school enrolling 50,000 or more students: Fall 2015

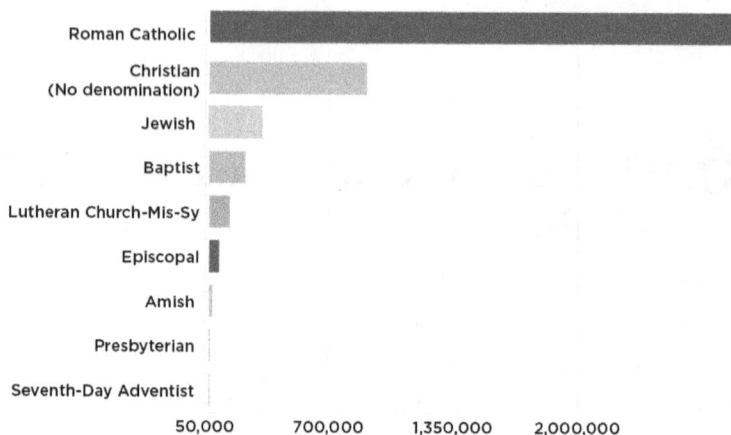

Roman Catholic
Christian (No denomination)
Jewish
Baptist
Lutheran Church-Mis-Sy
Episcopal
Amish
Presbyterian
Seventh-Day Adventist

50,000   700,000   1,350,000   2,000,000

Sources: U.S. Department of Education, National Center for Education Statistics, Private School Universe Survey (PSS), 2015-16.

Graphic by Jordan Morgan

decline, according to Georgetown University's Center for Applied Research in the Apostolate. It reported that Catholic elementary schools declined almost by half from 9,366 in 1970 to 4,903 in 2020. Catholic high schools were down from 1,986 to 1,199.

78 How many U.S. Catholic colleges are there?

According to the International Student there are 221 Catholic colleges and universities in the United States. Their 720,000 students are half the students enrolled in faith-based U.S. colleges and universities. They include five medical schools, 28 law schools and 25 schools

Number of U.S. Catholic school students

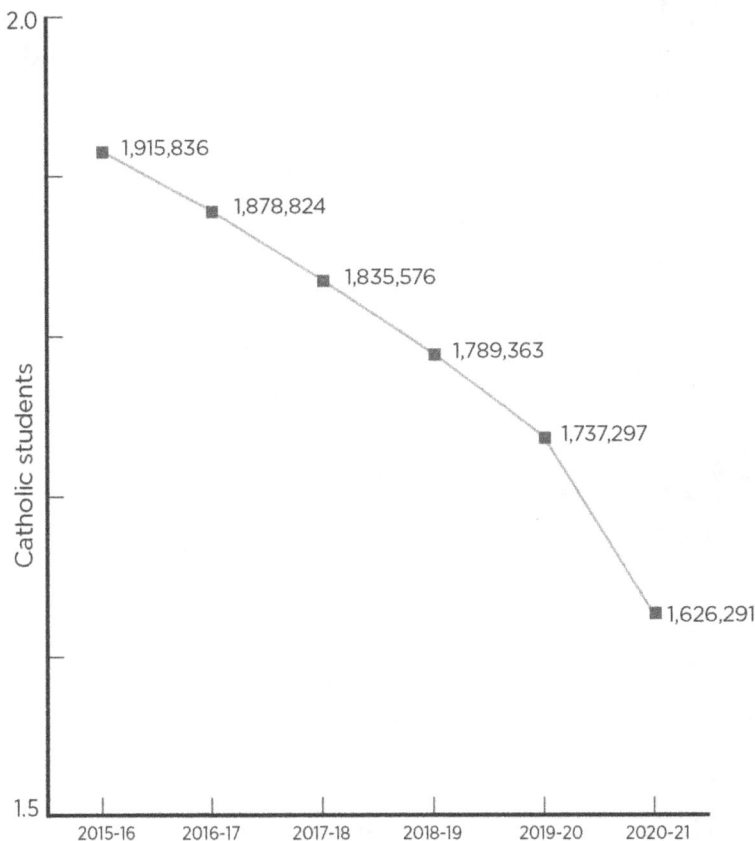

2.0

1,915,836
1,878,824
1,835,576
1,789,363
1,737,297
1,626,291

Catholic students

1.5

2015-16   2016-17   2017-18   2018-19   2019-20   2020-21

Source: NCEA.org/webinars   Graphic by Claire Chapin

of engineering. There are 128 schools for nursing,
163 for education, two for aviation and 14 women's
colleges. The largest Catholic universities are DePaul
University (Chicago), St. Leo University (Florida), St.
John's University-New York, St. Louis University, and
Georgetown University (Washington, D.C.). All have
enrollments of more than 20,000. Georgetown opened in
1789 as the first Catholic college in the United States.

79 How do Catholic schools differ from public schools?

The most notable difference is the practice of religion and instruction in a specific faith. The federal separation of church and state requires public schools to be neutral on religion. Financially, public schools are tax-supported. Catholic schools charge an average of $4,400 per elementary student, according to the U.S. bishops. Thirty percent of Catholic high schools are single gender. Non-Catholic students are 18.4 percent of the enrollment in Catholic K-12 schools.

80 Do Catholic children go to Sunday school?

Sunday school is a Protestant tradition that typically occurs before Sunday services. Catholics take several approaches. One is running Catholic schools that emphasize both general and religious education. Children who are not in Catholic schools may prepare for the sacraments with Continuing Christian Education. These may be held after school or on the weekend in churches or Catholic schools. A third kind of education occurs when young children are led out of Mass for a brief lesson or activity in a nearby room.

81 What were Indian boarding schools?

The Catholic Church operated these residential schools across North America. Sanctioned by U.S. and Canadian governments, the schools sought to assimilate Indigenous children into the dominant cultures. This meant extinguishing native religions, language, customs, clothing and grooming. Students were subjected to physical, mental, emotional and sexual abuse. Hundreds of children were reportedly buried in unmarked graves. According to the National Native American Boarding School Healing Coalition in Minneapolis, 30 states had 357 boarding schools with 60,000 children in 1926. U.S. Catholic religious orders ran 84 of the schools. In 2022, Pope Francis made what he called a "penitential pilgrimage" to Canada. In Alberta, Canada, he said, "I am sorry. I ask forgiveness, in particular, for the ways in which many members of the church and of religious communities cooperated, not least through their indifference, in projects of cultural destruction and forced assimilation..." He called the system cultural genocide. In 2023, the church repudiated 14th century texts that comprised the "doctrine of discovery." The texts appeared to sanction the colonization of the lands of any non-Christians. Those documents placed the people and the land under European Christian rulers. President Joe Biden issued a formal apology the next year for abuses by the U.S. government's role in boarding schools.

Abuse Scandals

82 How has the church addressed abuse scandals?

As in the rest of society, there have been scandals of sexual abuse of children for hundreds of years. In 1998, Pope John Paul II said the Catholic Church must "implore forgiveness" for its historical injustices. In 1985, the National Catholic Reporter became the first news organization to report extensively about sexual abuse by Catholic priests. In 2022, an inquest found that Pope Benedict, no longer in office, had failed to act against abusers when he was archbishop of Munich. In 2017, Pope Francis issued a decree holding accountable bishops who hid abuse. Francis also created a commission for the protection of minors. It was charged with evaluating seminaries and programs, and starting initiatives. Some, including at least one commission member, have criticized the efforts as insufficient and slow.

83 How widespread is sexual abuse by church clergy?

Child sexual abuse and coverups have involved thousands of clergy members and a larger, untold number of victims. Cases have been prosecuted for centuries. A 2002 Boston Globe project revealed that the Catholic Archdiocese of

Boston had covered up sexual abuse by clerics for decades. Lawsuits in other dioceses followed those revelations. In 2015, the Academy Award winning movie "Spotlight" told the story and was viewed by millions, including the pontifical commission on minors.

84 Has child sex abuse cost the church members?

Almost all U.S. religions are losing members. As for Catholics, four Pew Research surveys have attributed some of those losses to abuse scandals. Gallup polls support this. Pew asked ex-Catholics in 2008 whether they had left the church because of abuse scandals. About one quarter said this was so. In 2015, Pew asked former Catholics to say in their own words why they had left. About 4 percent mentioned the abuse scandal as the main reason. Three years later, Pew asked U.S. Catholics to rate Pope Francis' response to the scandal. Sixty-two percent said he was doing "only fair" or "poor." Thirty percent said he was doing an excellent or good job. The next year, the pope's positive ratings improved to 55 percent. However, in that survey, almost 70 percent of U.S. Catholics said abuse by Catholic clergy is ongoing. Gallup reported in 2019 that 37 percent of U.S. Catholics said news of abuse had led them to question whether they would remain in the church. In 2002, the proportion was 22 percent.

85 Have women religious been abused?

Following child abuse charges and the #MeToo movement, women religious spoke out. In 2018, an Associated Press investigation in Europe, Africa, Asia and South America described sexual and physical abuse of nuns and sisters by male clergy. In 2019, the Reuters news service reported that Pope Francis had acknowledged that priests and bishops had abused women religious. The church had not acknowledged this before.

Social Issues

86 How do Catholics feel about COVID-19 vaccinations?

The church lets Catholics decide for themselves. Pope Francis received the vaccine. He said this was an "act of love" and a "moral obligation" of caring for one's health. He said "ideological divides" about the vaccine were fueled by "baseless information or poorly documented facts." Studies showed Hispanic and White Catholics with the highest vaccination rates among religious groups. Some Catholics seek exemptions from vaccinations on religious grounds. Archbishop for the U.S. Military Services Timothy P. Broglio supported the vaccine but said people should not be forced to receive it.

87 What is the church's position on global warming?

In 2015, Pope Francis issued a 40,000-word encyclical letter "Laudato Si." It was the most comprehensive Vatican statement ever on environmentalism, ethics and faith. It emphasized the urgency of global warming and climate change. Pope Francis called on Catholics to be stewards of the Earth and encouraged them to live with their children's futures in mind. Eight years later, in 2023,

Pope Francis challenged, "We are now unable to halt the enormous damage we have caused. We barely have time to prevent even more tragic damage." His message singled out the United States. A 2022 Pew study found that highly religious American adults express much less concern than less religious people about global warming.

88 How does the church view suicide?

The "Catechism of the Catholic Church" states that suicide defies God's design and is immoral. However, it does not teach that people who take their lives are condemned or have sinned. According to the catechism, "We should not despair of the eternal salvation of persons who have taken their own lives. By ways known to him alone, God can provide the opportunity for salutary repentance. The church prays for persons who have taken their own lives." The catechism states that circumstances leading to suicide, such as mental illness, can "diminish the responsibility of the one committing suicide." The church no longer denies funerals and burials to people who die by suicide.

89 Is the church offering reparations for slavery?

One Catholic institution is. The church officially disapproved of slavery even as its institutions and members profited by it. The Society of Jesus says it saved Georgetown University in 1838 by selling 272 enslaved men, women and children to plantation owners. Rachel Swarns, a Carter Journalism Institute professor, documented the Georgetown case. She said, "the Catholic

Church established its foothold in the South and relied on plantations and slave labor to help finance the livelihoods of its priests and nuns, and to support its schools and religious projects." The Jesuits have pledged to raise $100 million for restitution. Descendants had sought $1 billion.

Money

90 How well off are U.S. Catholics financially?

Like the comparison on educational levels, U.S. Catholics mirrored the national average more closely than any other religion. This is Pew's breakdown of average household incomes for all U.S. households in 2015.

$100,000 or more	19%
$50,000-$99,999	26%
$30,000-$49,999	20%
$30,000 or less	35%

Catholic households had the same breakdown except their numbers were 36 percent in the lowest category and 19 percent in the $30,00-$49,999 category.

91 Do Catholics tithe?

The practice of giving 10 percent of one's treasure and time to church and community is not embedded in Catholic tradition. Some churches suggest parishioners give 5 percent of their money to the church and 5 percent to charity. Statistics on individual giving are not public. According to the Philanthropy Roundtable, Catholics give less than Latter-day Saints, however, Catholics play a major role in charitable work.

92 Where does Catholic charity go?

Charity is prominent in Catholic teaching and actions. The church provides money, services and volunteers around the United States and globally. The primary beneficiaries of the church's global network are health care and education. The Pontifical Council for the Pastoral Care of Health Care Workers reports that the church manages 26 percent of the world's healthcare facilities. Additionally, the church supports thousands of schools, easing demand for public education. Funds are also available in emergencies such as natural disasters. Catholic giving has many faces. These Catholic charities are in the Forbes list of 50 top charities with revenue figures for 2023:

Catholic Relief Services	$674 million
Catholic Medical Mission Board	$465 million
Cross Catholic Outreach	$384 million
Providence St. Joseph Outreach	$331 million

There are many Catholic charities at the regional, diocesan, or parish level.

93 How wealthy is the global Catholic Church?

This is unclear. The Wealth Record put the value of the Catholic Church at $30 billion. Canada's National Post tried to calculate the worth of the church and gave up, saying it is probably impossible even for the church to know. The Post wrote, "between the church's priceless art, land, gold and investments across the globe, it is one of the wealthiest institutions on Earth." In terms of annual income, the church's operations center, the Vatican, is becoming more transparent. It has been reporting annual budgets of about $350 million.

94 How much money has the abuse scandal cost the church?

This is hard to pin down. Many dioceses have made payments, and many cases have been settled privately. One estimate of fines, settlements and legal costs is $4 billion. Four of eight dioceses filed for bankruptcy in New York, where 9,000 suits were filed under the state's Child Victims Act. Penn State Law reported that 31 Catholic organizations had filed for Chapter 11 bankruptcy protection as of May 2022. In 2023, the Catholic Archdiocese of Baltimore filed for bankruptcy days before a new law allowed civil lawsuits over older acts of child sexual abuse. In late 2024, the Los Angeles archdiocese agreed to pay $880 million for clergy sexual abuse dating back decades. It was the largest settlement involving the Catholic Church and came on top of the archdiocese's earlier settlement of $740 million.

Politics

95 Is the church involved in politics?

Yes. The U.S. bishops' statement "Catholics in Political Life" reads, "The separation of church and state does not require division between belief and public action, between moral principles and political choices ..." The statement says separation "protects the right of believers and religious groups to practice their faith and act on their values in public life." The statement stresses interacting with lawmakers. Abortion is a key issue. Another is protecting the church's tax-exempt status.

Catholics, abortion and politics
% who think abortion should be ...

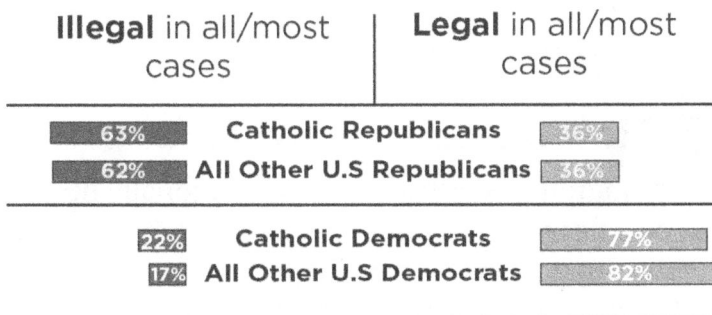

Illegal in all/most cases		Legal in all/most cases
63%	Catholic Republicans	36%
62%	All Other U.S Republicans	36%
22%	Catholic Democrats	77%
17%	All Other U.S Democrats	82%

Source: Pew Research Center | Graphic by Nicholas Simon

96 Does the Catholic Church have lobbyists?

Catholic groups and individuals dedicate time and money to influence state and national policy, court decisions and campaigns. Lobbyists include the conference of bishops, Network Advocates for Catholic Social Justice, archdioceses and dioceses. They support religious liberty, Catholic education, social development, international justice and peace, migration and refugees. They have opposed abortion and same-sex marriage. In 2019, NBC News reported that the church spent $10.6 million on lobbyists in eight northeastern states to prevent victims of clerical sex abuse from suing for damages. Sometimes, Catholic lobbyists are on opposite sides.

97 Does the Catholic Church endorse candidates?

Officially, church law opposes this. The church's tax-exempt status prohibits political endorsements. Church buildings are rarely used for campaigning. However, there are many instances of church leaders endorsing candidates for their positions on issues.

98 How do Catholics vote for president?

The Washington Post asked Catholics nationally how they voted just after they cast their ballots for president in 2020 and 2024. Support for Donald Trump grew substantially. In 2020, Catholics favored Trump over Joe Biden 52 percent to 47 percent. In 2024, Trump beat Kamala Harris 56 percent to 41 percent among Catholics.

The religious makeup of the 117th congress

House

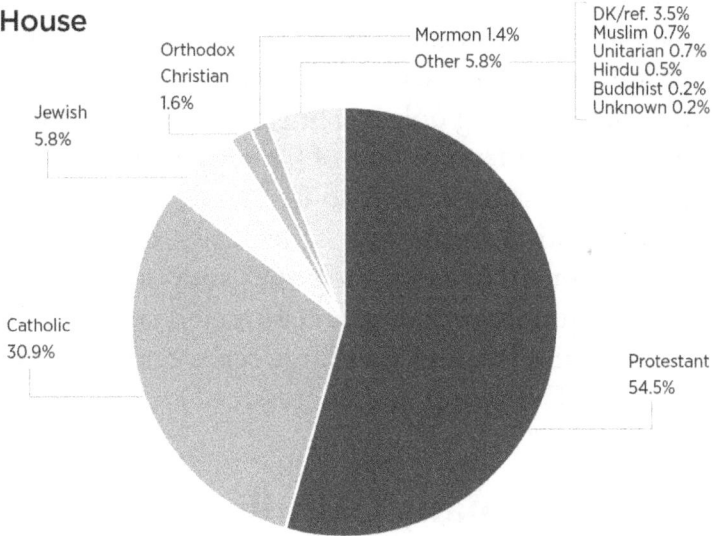

- Mormon 1.4%
- Other 5.8%
- DK/ref. 3.5%
- Muslim 0.7%
- Unitarian 0.7%
- Hindu 0.5%
- Buddhist 0.2%
- Unknown 0.2%
- Orthodox Christian 1.6%
- Jewish 5.8%
- Catholic 30.9%
- Protestant 54.5%

Senate

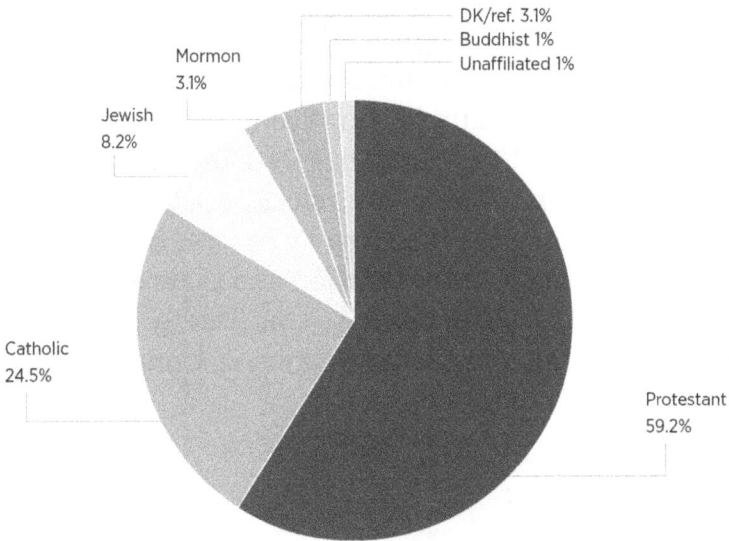

- DK/ref. 3.1%
- Buddhist 1%
- Unaffiliated 1%
- Mormon 3.1%
- Jewish 8.2%
- Catholic 24.5%
- Protestant 59.2%

Source: Pew Research Center   Graohic by Kayla McKaig

99 Does having a Catholic in the White House help the church?

There have been two Catholic presidents: John F. Kennedy and Joe Biden. Both had complex relationships with the church and its members. Catholics were divided on Biden. This is generally along political lines. U.S. bishops have spoken against Biden because of his support for abortion rights. There was an effort by some to have him barred from Communion. Some have called this a distraction and said Biden seemed to enjoy the pope's support. Kennedy, as the first Catholic president, encountered suspicion in the 1960s. Catholics now have large representations on the U.S. Supreme Court and in Congress.

100 How many Catholics are in Congress and on the Supreme Court?

According to Pew, Catholics comprised 28.2 percent of the 2025-2026 U.S. Congress. This compares to 20 percent of the U.S. adult population. Six of nine U.S. Supreme Court justices are Catholic. The Capitol Hill publication Roll Call reported that Catholics were underrepresented in government until Kennedy's election. "The number of Catholics in Congress has risen by roughly 50 percent since the Kennedy administration and in recent years," Roll Call said. "... Catholics have consistently been the single largest religious denomination in Congress."

Afterword

By Pat McCloskey, OFM

Catholicism is the way that many people live out their faith in Jesus Christ. It is first a relationship and only later content (a system of coordinated beliefs and practices).

Do two people on their first date try to reveal themselves completely to each other? Hardly. Those who attempt that will probably not have a second date. Relationships tend to grow gradually. A couple's need for information increases in proportion to the increasing depth of their relationship.

Faith is not like an on/off light switch. It's more like an adjustable rheostat. People can and must grow in their faith. The beliefs and practices that were very important to a 5-year-old will not be enough to sustain the faith of that same person at age 7, 35, 67 or 89. Faith-as-an-object can be lost like a wallet, credit card or TV remote. Faith-as-a-relationship must grow because we know that relationships either grow or wither; they rarely remain the same.

Many people see faith as a possession that belongs in a safety deposit box. That is impossible for faith-as-relationship. Only government bonds grow in locked boxes — and then only to a certain point as time passes. Faith as a relationship needs to be nurtured and stretched. People who prefer to think of faith primarily as a possession are in danger of having it become fossilized — and then "lost."

People join religious groups as adults or remain in the one their families chose for various reasons — some noble and others less so. I was born in 1948 and was probably in my teens before I ever heard someone use the expression "adult faith." Faith was simply faith, right? Did it need an adjective to modify it?

Women and men who resist the concept of "adult faith" may never develop one for themselves because they strongly approach life in either/or terms instead of using a both/and stance. Some situations are indeed either/or (saving a child about to be hit by a car), but other parts of life are more both/and (how a person moves from teen years to adulthood, for example).

Religious language and practices can sometimes give a false sense of security. Biblical prophets frequently warn about that. Opening oneself to God's grace and cooperating generously with it may seem entirely too uncertain.

We do not, however, simply grow as individuals; we also grow as members of a community of faith. That can be messy at times, but it is always real.

The Gospel of St. Luke tells us that Jesus grew in wisdom, age and grace (2:53). The same evangelist also tells us that Mary, the mother of Jesus, "remembered all these things and pondered them in her heart" (2:19 and 2:52).

Pat McCloskey is the Franciscan editor of St. Anthony Messenger magazine for which he writes the "Ask a Franciscan" column. He has written extensively. His most recent book is *Day by Day: Through the Year with Francis of Assisi* (Franciscan Media), also available as an audiobook. His work is available through Franciscan Media, a ministry of the Franciscan friars of St. John the Baptist Province at franciscanmedia.org. The print and online monthly St. Anthony Messenger has been published since 1893.

Photograph of Pat McCloskey
by Frank Gutbrod

Discussion and Reflection

This guide is only a first step. We hope you take the next one. That can be honest conversations with Catholics. They could be friends, neighbors or co-workers with whom you have never really had a conversation about faith. We hope talking leads to greater understanding and a fuller friendship.

Another way to explore can be through a group discussion. Ideally, this will include one or more Catholics. No two people have the same understanding or experience. For the best discussion, have everyone read this guide ahead of time. Every answer in the guide can be explored in greater depth. Expect disagreements and many more questions. All we can do in this simple guide is to answer some basic questions and help people feel comfortable asking questions.

Here are questions to think or talk about.

1. Millions of U.S. Catholics seem comfortable with accommodating the religion to suit their lives and not adapting their lives to the church. Does this help the church or hurt it? Is this a good approach? Is it desirable to find more common ground?

2. Many Catholics have left the church over sex abuse scandals involving priests and children. But millions of Catholics who disapprove of these activities are sticking with the church. How do people who have major differences with the church remain?

3. Many U.S. Catholics say they personally oppose abortion but do not believe there should be laws against it. What values are they reconciling with this position? Would this rationale work for you? Why or why not?

4. One of the fastest growing faith groups in the United States is people who are religiously unaffiliated. Many are ex-Catholics. The church is evangelizing former members. How best can that be done?

5. The Catholic Church, even as it evangelizes for people to join it, promotes ecumenical respect for other religions. It seeks worldwide unity and cooperation, even as it seeks to bring in members. How can the church do both?

6. The Catholic Church has very few religious roles for women, even in the face of a growing priest shortage. How would the Catholic Church be hurt or benefit by allowing women to be ordained, say Mass and perform Holy Eucharist?

7. Pope Francis became the first pope from the Western Hemisphere and the first from South America. His appointments have elevated cardinals from many more countries. The College of Cardinals, which had been primarily European, is now less than 40 percent European. Asia-Pacific representation has doubled to almost 20 percent and sub-Saharan African representation rose from 9 percent to 12 percent. How might the college's selection of a pope change the direction of the church? How might it influence the selection of future popes? What might it do to Pope Francis' legacy?

8. Large Catholic presences in the White House, Congress and the Supreme Court have raised questions about Rome's influence over Washington, D.C. Are there signs of church control? Should there be some kind of counterbalance? What would that look like?

9. Under U.S. rules for the separation of church and state, Catholic churches do not pay some taxes. U.S. bishops say this separation both "protects the right of believers and religious groups to practice their faith and act on their values in public life." Should religious institutions' freedom from taxes require them to stay out of politics? Or should the freedom to be politically active carry the responsibility to pay taxes?

10. The Catholic Church educates millions of children, including non-Catholic children, who might otherwise attend taxpayer-funded schools. While Catholic schools can receive money for some services, churches are not entitled to reimbursement for most expenses. Should that be changed? How?

11. Some Catholic churches are ornate with statues and paintings of saints. The images are meant to be inspirational, not idols. Muslim mosques have for centuries excluded imagery of people and animals, regarding them as a distraction from God and a form of polytheism. What are the merits of each philosophy?

12. People sometimes wonder about how Catholics regard the Virgin Mary. The church says Mary is not a god or divine, but venerates her above other figures. Is it a problem when one figure becomes more important than most others? Why or why not?

13. Some people object to being called "cafeteria Catholics" because they follow some church rules but not others. Can religion be à la carte? Or is it OK for people to claim a religion they observe selectively?

Resources

There are whole books on pretty much every topic in this guide. There is extensive content published online by the Catholic Church. That includes the Vatican's website at vatican.va/content/vatican/en.html and the United States Catholic Conference of Bishops at usccb.org.

There is content from Catholic dioceses and religious orders. Leading Catholic book publishers, which post their lists online, include Ignatius Press, Sophia Institute Press, TAN books, Ascension Press, Angelus Press. Loyola Press, Liturgical Press and Paraclete Press.

Dozens of Catholic-oriented publishers, both church-affiliated and independent, cover the global church and the U.S. church from every point of Catholic and political ideology. There are even differences of interpretation among Catholic religious orders. Almost 175 dioceses publish Catholic magazines, and there are about 20 more magazines, which tend to be larger, that are independent.

For 360-degree understanding, read what different Catholic sources say about the same issue. Publication names and titles are usually not a clue to politics, so look for how they describe their funding and editorial point of view.

U.S. Catholic magazines include America (Jesuit), The Angelus (Los Angeles), Catholic Digest, Catholic Standard

(Archdiocese of Washington), National Catholic Reporter, Catholic Journal, Commonweal (politics and culture), Faith Magazine (Lansing, Michigan), Glenmary Challenge (small towns) Liguorian (Denver), Maryknoll (missions), St. Anthony Messenger (Franciscans), Today's Catholic (northern Indiana), U.S. Catholic (social justice) and Crux (independent).

And these are a few books:

Barron, Robert and John L. Allen Jr. *To Light a Fire on the Earth: Proclaiming the Gospel in a Secular Age*. New York City: Image Books. 2017.

Catechism of the Catholic Church (2nd ed.) Vatican City: Libreria Editrice Vaticana. 2020. Free online: https://www.vatican.va/archive/ENG0015/_INDEX.HTM

Cole, Casey. *Called: What Happens After Saying Yes to God*. Cincinnati: Franciscan Media. 2018.

Cole, Casey. *Let Go: Seven Stumbling Blocks to Christian Discipleship*. Cincinnati: Franciscan Media. 2020.

Donnelly, Elizabeth and Russ Petrus. *Catholic Women Preach: Raising Voices, Renewing the Church*, three volumes. Maryknoll: Orbis. 2022-2024.

Faggilo, Massimo. *Joe Biden and Catholicism in the United States*. Worcester: Bayard. 2021.

Fialka, John J. *Sisters: Catholic Nuns and the Making of America*. New York City: St. Martin's Griffin. 2004.

Francois, Susan Rose and Juliet Mousseau. *Reseeding Religious Life through Global Sisterhood*. Collegeville: Liturgical Press. 2024.

Guillot, Lawrence B., Thomas C. Fox (foreword) and Bill Mitchell (afterword). *Beacon of Justice, Community, and Hope: How NCR (National Catholic Reporter) Has Sustained Independent Journalism from Vatican II to Pope Francis*. Canton: Read the Spirit Books. 2024.

McCloskey, Pat. *Ask a Franciscan: Answers to Catholic Questions*. Cincinnati: St. Anthony Messenger Press. 2011.

McCloskey, Pat. *Peace and Good: Through the Year with Francis of Assisi*. Cincinnati: Franciscan Media. 2020.

McGreevy, John T. *Catholicism: A Global History from the French Revolution to Pope Francis*. New York City: W. W. Norton & Company. 2022.

Montemurri, Patricia. *Immaculate Heart of Mary Sisters of Michigan*. Mt. Pleasant: Arcadia. 2020.

National Catholic Reporter. *Global Sisters Report*. https://www.globalsistersreport.org/

O'Loughlin, Michael J. *Hidden Mercy: AIDS, Catholics, and the Untold Stories of Compassion in the Face of Fear*. Minneapolis: Broadleaf Books. 2021.

O'Malley, John. *What Happened at Vatican II*. Cambridge: Harvard University Press. 2022.

Pope Francis. *A Better World: Reflections on Peace and Fraternity*. Huntington: Our Sunday Visitor. 2022.

Pope, Charles. *Catholic and Curious: Your Questions Answered*. Huntington: Our Sunday Visitor. 2018.

Reid, Barbara E. *Taking Up the Cross: New Testament Interpretations through Latina and Feminist Eyes*. Revised. Philadelphia: Fortress Press. 2007.

Religion Newswriters. *Reporting on Religion 2: A Stylebook on Journalism's Best Beat*. Westerville: Religion Newswriters. 2007.

Rock, Paul and Bill Tammeus. *Jesus, Pope Francis, and a Protestant Walk into a Bar: Lessons for the Christian Church*. Louisville: Westminster John Knox Press. 2015.

Weigel, George. *To Sanctify the World: The Vital Legacy of Vatican II*. New York City: Basic Books. 2022.

Our Story

The 100 Questions and Answers series springs from the idea that good journalism should increase cross-cultural competence and understanding. Most of our guides are created by Michigan State University journalism students.

We use journalistic interviews to surface the simple, everyday questions that people have about each other but might be afraid to ask. We use research and reporting to get the answers and then put them where people can find them, read them and learn about each other.

These cultural competence guides are meant to be conversation starters. We want people to use these guides to get some baseline understanding and to feel comfortable asking more questions. We put a resources section in every guide we make and we arrange community conversations. While the guides can answer questions in private, they are meant to spark discussions.

Making these has taught us that people are not that different from each other. People share more similarities than differences. We all want the same things for ourselves and for our families. We want to be accepted, respected and understood.

Please email your thoughts and suggestions to series editor Joe Grimm at joe.grimm@gmail.com, at the Michigan State University School of Journalism.

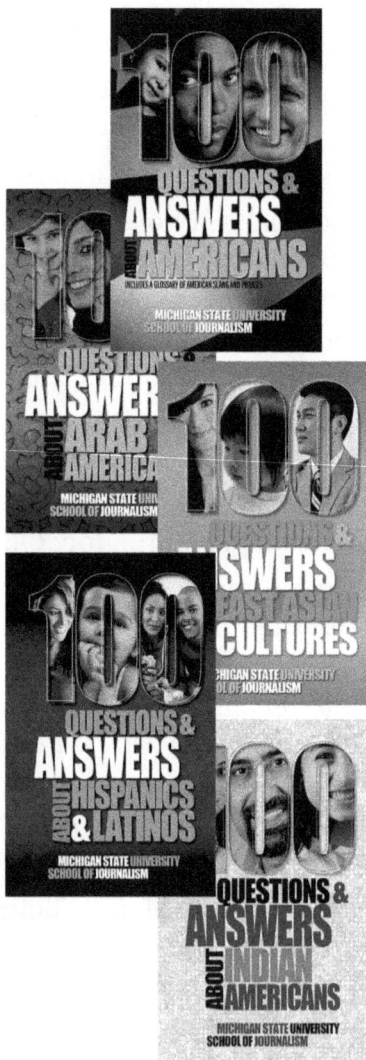

Related Books

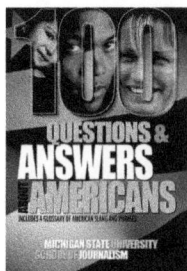

100 Questions and Answers About Americans
Michigan State University School of Journalism, 2013

This guide answers some of the first questions asked by newcomers to the United States. Questions represent dozens of nationalities coming from Africa, Asia, Australia, Europe and North and South America. Good for international students, guests and new immigrants.

ISBN: 978-1-939880-20-8

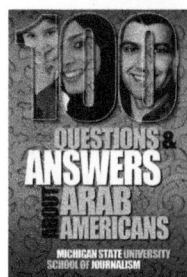

100 Questions and Answers About Arab Americans
Michigan State University School of Journalism, 2014

The terror attacks of Sept. 11, 2001, propelled these Americans into a difficult position where they are victimized twice. The guide addresses stereotypes, bias and misinformation. Key subjects are origins, religion, language and customs. A map shows places of national origin.

ISBN: 978-1-939880-56-7

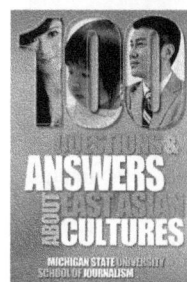

100 Questions and Answers About East Asian Cultures
Michigan State University School of Journalism, 2014

Large university enrollments from Asia prompted this guide as an aid for understanding cultural differences. The focus is on people from China, Japan, Korea and Taiwan and includes Mongolia, Hong Kong and Macau. The guide includes history, language, values, religion, foods and more.

ISBN: 978-939880-50-5

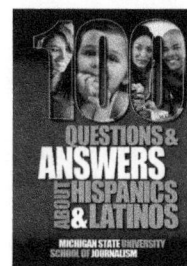

100 Questions and Answers About Hispanics & Latinos
Michigan State University School of Journalism, 2014

This group became the largest ethnic minority in the United States in 2014 and this guide answers many of the basic questions about it. Questions were suggested by Hispanics and Latinos. Includes maps and charts on origin and size of various Hispanic populations.

ISBN: 978-1-939880-44-4

Print and ebooks available on Amazon.com and other retailers.

Related Books

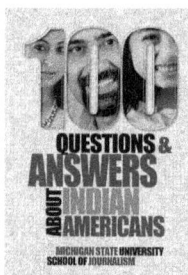

100 Questions and Answers About Indian Americans
Michigan State University School of Journalism, 2013

In answering questions about Indian Americans, this guide also addresses Pakistanis, Bangladeshis and others from South Asia. The guide covers religion, issues of history, colonization and national partitioning, offshoring and immigration, income, education, language and family.

ISBN: 978-1-939880-00-0 m

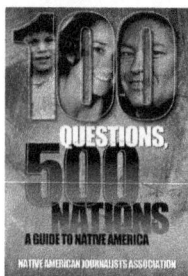

100 Questions, 500 Nations: A Guide to Native America
Michigan State University School of Journalism, 2014

This guide was created in partnership with the Native American Journalists Association. The guide covers tribal sovereignty, treaties and gaming, in addition to answers about population, religion, U.S. policies and politics. The guide includes the list of federally recognized tribes.

ISBN: 978-1-939880-38-3

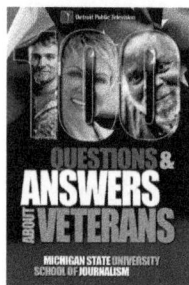

100 Questions and Answers About Veterans
Michigan State University School of Journalism, 2015

This guide treats the more than 20 million U.S. military veterans as a cultural group with distinctive training, experiences and jargon. Graphics depict attitudes, adjustment challenges, rank, income and demographics. Includes six video interviews by Detroit Public Television.

ISBN: 978-1-942011-00-2

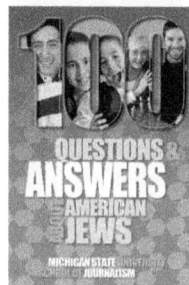

100 Questions and Answers About American Jews
Michigan State University School of Journalism, 2016

We begin by asking and answering what it means to be Jewish in America. The answers to these wide-ranging, base-level questions will ground most people and set them up for meaningful conversations with Jewish acquaintances.

ISBN: 978-1-942011-22-4

news.jrn.msu.edu/culturalcompetence

Related Books

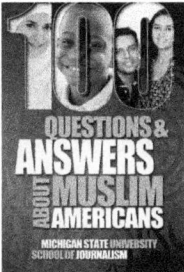

100 Questions and Answers About Muslim Americans
Michigan State University School of Journalism, 2014

This guide was done at a time of rising intolerance in the United States toward Muslims. The guide describes the presence of this religious group around the world and inside the United States. It includes audio on how to pronounce some basic Muslim words.

ISBN: 978-1-939880-79-6

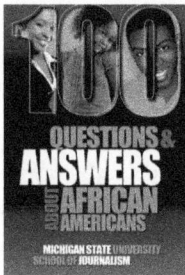

100 Questions and Answers About African Americans
Michigan State University School of Journalism, 2016

Learn about the racial issues that W.E.B. DuBois said in 1900 would be the big challenge for the 20th century. This guide explores Black and African American identity, history, language, contributions and more. Learn more about current issues in American cities and campuses.

ISBN: 978-1-942011-19-4

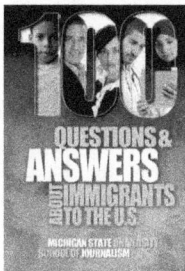

100 Questions and Answers About Immigrants to the U.S.
Michigan State University School of Journalism, 2016

This simple, introductory guide answers 100 of the basic questions people ask about U.S. immigrants and immigration in everyday conversation. It has answers about identity, language, religion, culture, customs, social norms, economics, politics, education, work, families and food.

ISBN: 978-1-934879-63-4

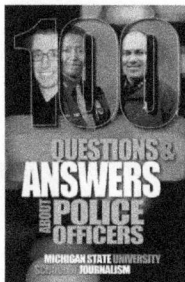

100 Questions and Answers about Police Officers
Michigan State University School of Journalism, 2018

This simple, introductory guide answers 100 of the basic questions people ask about police officers, sheriff's deputies, public safety officers and tribal police. It focuses on policing at the local level, where procedures vary from coast to coast. The guide includes a resource about traffic stops.

ISBN: 978-1-64180-013-6

Print and ebooks available on Amazon.com and other retailers.

Related Books

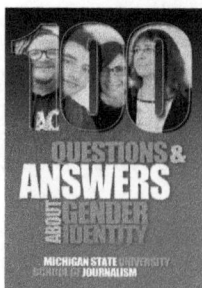

100 Questions and Answers About Gender Identity
Michigan State University School of Journalism, 2017

The guide is written for anyone who wants quick answers to basic, introductory questions about transgender people. It is a starting point people who want to get a fast grounding in the facts.

ISBN: 978-1-641-800-02-0

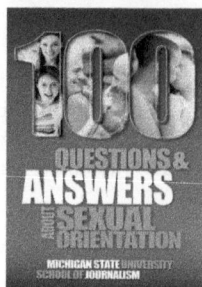

100 Questions and Answers About Sexual Orientation
Michigan State University School of Journalism, 2018

This clear, introductory guide answers 100 of the basic questions people ask about people who are lesbian, gay, bisexual or who have other sexual orientations. The questions come from interviews with people who say these are issues they frequently get asked about or wish people knew more about.

ISBN: 978-1-641-800-27-3

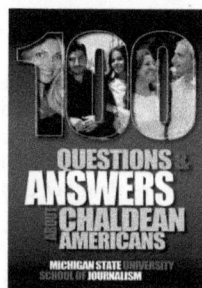

100 Questions and Answers About Chaldean Americans
Michigan State University School of Journalism, 2019

This guide has sections on identity, language, religion, culture, customs, social norms, economics, politics, education, work, families and food. It is written for those who want authoritative answers to basic, questions about this immigrant group from Iraq.

ISBN: 978-1-934-879-63-4

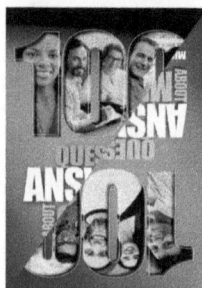

100 Questions and Answers About Gen X Plus
100 Questions and Answers About Millennials
Michigan State University School of Journalism, 2019

This is a double guide in the Bias Busters series. It is written for those who want authoritative answers about these important generations and how we all work together.

ISBN: 978-1-641-800-47-1

news.jrn.msu.edu/culturalcompetence

Related Books

True Border: 100 Questions and Answers About the U.S.-Mexico Frontera
Borderzine: Reporting Across Fronteras, 2020

This guide was developed by the University of Texas/Borderzine for the Bias Busters cultural competence series. The guide is written for people who want authoritative answers about the U.S.-Mexico border region and get up to speed quickly on this important topic.

ISBN: 978-1-641-800-60-0

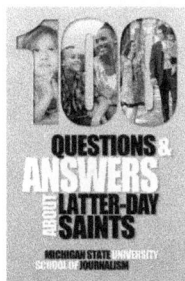

100 Questions and Answers About Latter-day Saints
Michigan State University School of Journalism, 2020

This guide is written for those who want authoritative answers to basic questions about the Latter-day Saints faith. It relies extensively on the Church of Jesus Christ of Latter-day Saints writings and suggests resources for greater depth.

ISBN: 978-1-641-800-90-7

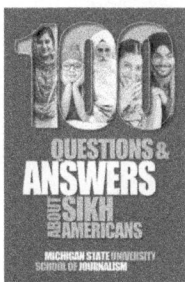

100 Questions and Answers About Sikh Americans
Michigan State University School of Journalism, 2022

Sikhism is the fifth largest religion in the world. It is a young religion, having been founded in 1469. It has been in the United States for almost 150 years, but is still relatively unknown. The questions in this guide were created by interviewing Sikhs.

ISBN: 978-1-641-801-43-0

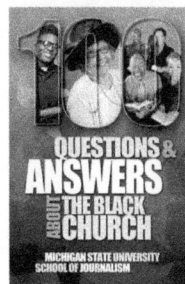

100 Questions and Answers About The Black Church
Michigan State University School of Journalism, 2022

Forged in the furnace of U.S. segregation, the Black Church is the pillar of African American communities across the country. This guide answers the call that TIME magazine raised in a headline, "To understand America, you need to understand the Black Church."

ISBN: 978-1-641-801-55-3

Print and ebooks available on Amazon.com and other retailers.

Related Books

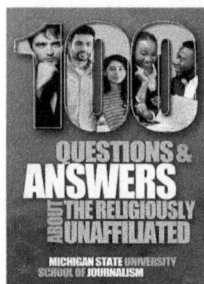

100 Questions and Answers About the Religiously Unaffiliated
Michigan State University School of Journalism, 2024

Sometimes generally referred to as "the nones," agnostics, atheists, humanists, freethinkers, secularists and skeptics compose one of the fastest growing faith categories in the United States. Some people face discrimination as nonbelievers, despite their varied and strong beliefs, values and morals.

ISBN: 978-1-641-801-66-9

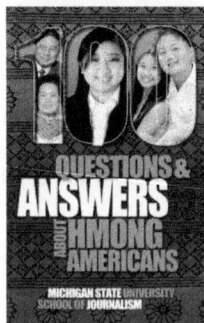

100 Questions and Answers About Hmong Americans
Michigan State University School of Journalism, 2024

In the 50 years since the CIA's secret war against Communists in Vietnam ended, Hmong Americans have built new lives in a country they fought for, even though they did not belong to it. When the United States ended its military involvement in Southeast Asia in 1975, it left its secret allies defenseless among enemies in a hostile land. Neither the Hmong people nor their U.S. hosts were prepared for the change.

ISBN: 978-1-641-801-92-8

www.ingramcontent.com/pod-product-compliance
Lightning Source LLC
Chambersburg PA
CBHW022035090426
42741CB00007B/1076